the new
complete
tourist
guide

Florence

*12 Itineraries
the Monuments
the Museums
the Medici
the Curiosities*

TEMPO LIBERO

bysillabe

Florentine 12 Itineraries

© 2007 **s i l l a b e** s.r.l.
Livorno
www.sillabe.it   info@sillabe.it

Managing Editor: *Maddalena Paola Winspeare*
Texts and curiosities (☺): *Ethel Santacroce*
Additional material (↯): *Monica Guarraccino*
Graphic Design: *Laura Belforte*
Editing: *Giulia Bastianelli*
Translation: *Emily Ligniti, Sara Gioia Traduzioni*
Cartography: *DBMap, Firenze*
Photo Credits: *Archivio Sillabe: Foto R. Bardazzi, P. Nannoni, N. Orsi Battaglini, Rabatti & Domingie, G. Valsecchi, S. Zinelli*

The publisher is at the disposal of the copyright holders of images from unidentified sources.

ISBN 978-88-8347-352-4

(*)   panoramic view
(☺) curiosity
(↯) additional material
(🖑) not to be missed!
Museums . . . in italics

A BIT of HISTORY

Perspective map known as "della Catena," *"Firenze com'era"* Museum

Though its origins are Etruscan, Florence was actually founded in 59 B.C. by the Romans who built an encampment along the Arno River called *Florentia*.

You can still make out the ancient *cardus* and *decumanus* in Piazza della Repubblica near the Column of Abundance between Via Roma-Via Calimala (*cardus maximus*) and Strozzi-Via del Corso (*decumanus maximus*). Even the city's partition into 4 historical sections dates back to Roman times.

During the barbarian invasions, Florence was besieged by the Ostrogoths (405), though its towering walls kept the invaders from entering the city. Then came the Byzantines (535) and finally the Goths, who captured Florence in 541.

During the Carolingians (8th cent.), the city became part of the Holy Roman Empire. It was later controlled by Countess Matilde of Canossa. In 1115, when the Countess died, Florence was able to transform itself into an independent commune governed by influential rich merchants, powerful members of the clergy, and prominent noble families.

The city was often divided between two factions: the Guelphs (loyal to the Pope) and the Ghibellines (supporters of the Emperor). These two factions repeatedly clashed (the Ghibelline victory at Montaperti in 1260 is emblematic).

In 1289, the Guelphs were able to defeat Arezzo at Campaldino. This decisive battle resulted in Florence's complete domination over the other cities in Tuscany.

Despite the mutually destructive rivalry between these two factions, Florence began its climb to the top thanks to its famous wool and silk trade.

4

If you can, try to stop by the Medici villas outside Florence. **7 VILLA PETRAIA** (Via della Petraia, 40) and **8 VILLA DI CASTELLO** (Via di Castello, 47) were purchased by the Medici during the 16th century; here Tribolo created the marvelous three-level gardens, of which the Italian-style ones are considered the most beautiful in Europe. The splendid **9 VILLA MEDICI OF POGGIO A CAIANO** (Piazza de' Medici, 12, Poggio a Caiano) (✋), which still maintains its original medieval fortress structure surrounded by a ring of walls with small towers at the corners, is famous for having been Lorenzo the Magnificent's preferred villa. In fact, he had it refurbished in the classical style with a Greek temple-shaped entrance. Try to visit the museum located inside the villa.

Giambologna, Apennine, *Villa Demidoff Park*

MEDICI BIOGRAPHIES

The Medici and Florence—two names that are inextricably linked to each other. Beginning in the Middle Ages, but more specifically between the Renaissance and the 18th century, the personality, culture, and sensibility of the Medici sovereigns united itself to the city's vitality, nurtured by the people who lived here: artists, poets, men of letters as well as artisans and workers who were able to interpret a unique vision of the world that was oftentimes innovative and visionary. They are responsible for the breathtaking art we all admire today, and have created one of the world's greatest city-museums.

The first Medici who played an important role in the city's history was **Giovanni d'Averardo**, known as "**di Bicci**" (Florence ? 1360–1429). He established the most powerful dynasty in Florence's history and was able to lay the foundations for a Republic that paid attention to the needs of the middle and lower classes.

In 1413, Giovanni became the trustee of anti-Pope John XXIII. In this role, he was able to pave the way to his family's economic rise and to co-participate in the business dealings of the Curia. After having opened various money exchange branches in Venice, Rome, and Naples, in 1421 he was elected Gonfalonier of Florence, thereby giving life to a policy that was aimed at obtaining almost absolute power by way of consent from the middle and lower classes. A promoter of the arts, Giovanni, in 1421, entrusted Brunelleschi with building "the Sacristy and a chapel" inside the Church of S. Lorenzo by sponsoring a part of the transept and the longitudinal section connected to the ancient basilica. In this way, Giovanni began the radical transformation of what would become the private church of the Medici. This project would be completed by his heirs.

Giovanni's successor was **Cosimo**, his son, known as **the Elder** or "Pater Patriae" (Florence 1389–1464). Cosimo was very intelligent and had a striking personality, which he expressed in his business dealings and intellectual interests, especially in his appreciation of philosophy. An opponent of Florentine aristocracy, he was forced into exile from 1432 to 1434, but when he returned he led the Medici family to complete dominion of the city and the entire region of Tuscany. A promoter of the *Platonic Academy* and a collector of the first core of codices that would later constitute the *Medici-Laurentian Library*, Cosimo was an art lover as well. The friend of B. Angelico and P. Uccello, he was particularly fascinated with Donatello. In fact, he commissioned this artist with the stucco decorations and the bronze doors in the Old Sacristy and the (unfinished) bronze pulpits in S. Lorenzo, in addition to the statues of *David* and *Judith and Holofernes*. Mich-

Michelozzo, Medici Chapel, S. Croce Basilica
Medici coat-of-arms, Chapel of Princes

elozzo was Cosimo's preferred architect. He was asked to build Palazzo Medici on Via Larga, the Badia Fiesolana, the convent of S. Marco, the Novitiate Chapel in S. Croce, and the Church of the Annunziata.

Piero the Gouty (Florence 1416–1469) came to power at the age of 48 and, despite some initial difficulties, he was able, starting in 1466, to win back support for his short-lived reign, which lasted a mere five years. He had been sent abroad by his father to follow the family business at the most important courts of the age. The King of France granted him the right to place the *fleur-de-lys* upon his family's coat-of-arms. A good scholar of Latin, Piero loved the decorative arts, which he enthusiastically collected. Some of his favorite painters included D. Veneziano and B. Gozzoli, who was commissioned with the chapel of the Palazzo Medici. He admired L. della Robbia for the preciousness of his majolicas and the inventiveness with which he used marble and glazed terracotta. He also praised Michelozzo, who was asked to build the small temple in SS. Annunziata and the Crucifix Chapel in S. Miniato al Monte.

Under **Lorenzo**, known by his contemporaries as **the Magnificent** (Florence 1449–1492), Florence flourished and became, thanks to extraordinary patronage, the "new Athens." Despite the conspiracy on the part of his enemies (especially Luca Pitti) who tried to eliminate the dynasty and the difficult political crisis when Papal and Neapolitan troops (1479) arrived in the city, Lorenzo was able to react with great skill. His talent for mediating allowed him to quickly form an alliance with the King of Naples, Ferrante, and to put an end to this turbulent situation. Lorenzo attended the *Platonic Academy* and was a refined man of

Botticelli, Adoration of the Magi, *Uffizi*

letters. He wrote works of all kinds in vulgate and was a great patron of the arts. He carried on the patronage of his predecessors and collaborated with many artists. Some of his most favorite artists included A. del Verrocchio (Leonardo da Vinci and Perugino trained in his workshop that created objects in gold, sculptures, and paintings), who made the *Baptism of Christ*, the statue *David* (for the villa of Careggi, today housed in the Bargello Museum), and the innovative *Putto with Dolphin*, presently found in Palazzo Vecchio. He also admired Filippino Lippi, whose reputation among his contemporaries was boosted thanks to Lorenzo. G. da Sangallo was the Magnificent's preferred architect and interpreter of the aristocratic and neo-platonic ideals in vogue in Florence during those years. This architect was able to translate the basic principles of the philosophy of the age into the ideal of perfect forms. This is especially evident in the works commissioned by Lorenzo: the Church of S. Maria delle Carceri in Prato, the sacristy of S. Spirito, and the Villa di Poggio a Caiano.

Piero, known as **the Unfortunate** (Florence 1472?–Gaeta 1503), Lorenzo's son, reigned for just two years (1492–1494). Even though he, too, was educated and erudite, Piero was nothing in comparison to his father. In fact, he committed a series of grave political mistakes. He was forced to leave Florence with his brothers Giovanni, future Pope Leo X, and Giuliano. After the Medici fled from the city, the family's immense patrimony, made up of art objects, furnishings, and priceless manuscripts, was looted by the enraged masses. This brought about the dispersion of a veritable treasure-

trove, collected during the golden age of Florence's art and culture. The Medici returned to Florence in 1512.

Giuliano (Florence 1479–1516), elected **Duke of Nemours** by the King of France, ruled for one year (until 1513). However, he was praised and admired for his skill as a mediator and for his honesty. In 1513, he moved to Rome with the title Gonfalonier of the Papal Army—a position he was given by his brother Giovanni who had been elected Pope Leo x (Florence 1475-Rome 1521). Giuliano was buried in the New Sacristy of S. Lorenzo. His sepulchral effigy was made by Michelangelo.

Lorenzo Duke of Urbino (Florence 1492–1519), son of Piero the Unfortunate, was initially loyal to the political policies of the Medici pope, Leo x (in fact, this pope granted Lorenzo many privileges). However, he soon distanced himself, thereby revealing his insatiable ambitiousness.

The illegitimate son of Giulio de' Medici (Pope Clement vii, Florence 1478–Rome 1534), **Alessandro** (Florence 1511–1537) acted as the city's first duke. Shrewd and revengeful, he became a tyrant. He married Margherita, the daughter of Emperor Charles v, but was assassinated a few months later by his cousin Lorenzino, nicknamed "Lorenzaccio."

After Alessandro's untimely death, the responsibility of ruling the city fell into the hands of the very young **Cosimo i** (Florence 1519–1574). The son of Giovanni of the Black Bands, he chose to ally himself with the Emperor. In 1539, he wed Eleanor, the daughter of the Viceroy of Naples, Pedro of Toledo. Together with his wife, he left his palace on Via Larga and moved to Palazzo della Signoria. During his reign, Cosimo was able to consolidate the Duchy's political and economic policies. He managed to almost double the size of his domain when he acquired Siena. He also created a war fleet, established the Ordine Militare di S. Stefano, opened silver mines in Pietrasanta and marble quarries in Carrara, was allowed to process alum in Piombino, and set up a strategic garrison in Portoferraio.

Cosimo reaped the rewards of his actions in 1569 when Pope Pious v gave him the title of Grand Duke. But all these accomplishments were outshined by the saddest defeat of all: in 1562, his children Giovanni and Garzia died from a terrible fever. His beloved wife Eleanor followed shortly after.

Deprived of his wife who had been an intelligent and loyal advisor that helped him with her riches and supported him politically by means of her father's precious interventions with the pope, in 1564 Cosimo decided to withdraw from public life. He appointed his son Francesco as successor.

Cosimo was also an exceptional patron of the arts. In 1547, he commissioned the Loggia of the Mercato Nuovo and in 1548, he decided to open the Medici-Laurentian Library (Giorgio Vasari was asked to complete the work Michelangelo had started) to the public. In 1554, Cellini's *Perseus* was placed under the Loggia della Signoria. In 1555, he entrusted G. Vasari with the task of transforming Palazzo della Signoria into a residence fit for a prince. In 1560, Vasari was asked to build the Uffizi and its Corridor (today known as Vasari's Corridor) that united Palazzo Vecchio with Palazzo Pitti, which was purchased by Eleanor in 1549 and enlarged by B. Ammannati. In 1563, Cosimo founded the Accademia delle Arti e del Disegno, which is the first art academy in Europe.

Moreover, this Grand Duke changed Tuscany from an architectural point of view as he commissioned fortresses and fortified structures throughout the entire territory to the most prominent military architects of the age. His last public commission was the cycle of paintings for the dome in the Duomo. Vasari was entrusted with this task in 1574, but neither Cosimo nor the artist was able to see the finished dome since both died that very same year.

Cosimo's son, **Francesco I** (Florence 1541–1587) acted as regent until his father died, and governed from 1574 to 1587. Bashful and reticent, he repressed a conspiracy against himself on the part of the main families in Florence. As a result, hostilities increased. Francesco tried to continue with Cosimo's line of action, maintaining good

relationships with Spain and the Empire. However, he always preferred his great passions to politics: science and alchemy. In fact, he conducted many studies in pharmacology and physics.

Francesco's name is inextricably tied to that of Bianca Cappello, an extraordinarily beautiful Venetian woman. The Grand Duke loved her so much that he publicly boasted of their relationship while he was still married to Arch Duchess Giovanna of Austria. In 1578, two months after Giovanna died, Bianca finally became his legitimate wife and Grand Duchess of Tuscany. Francesco and Bianca remained together until they passed away. In fact, Francesco died a few short hours before Bianca on October 21, 1587 in their villa at Poggio a Caiano.

His so-called *Studiolo* is famous for its artistic quality and originality. Francesco wanted it to be located near the Salone dei Cinquecento in Palazzo Vecchio. In order to build this small study, inspired by the bonds between natural elements and human artifice according to the fundamental principles of alchemy, the Grand Duke called upon artists such as Vasari, Bronzino, Ammannati, and Giambologna who created a veritable "Wunderkammer," or room of wonders, embellished with splendid painted panels behind which small cabinets and treasure-troves hid rare and curious objects. Moreover, Francesco was very passionate about rock crystal, semi-precious stones, porcelain, and ceramic, which he even experimented with at times. His preferred artist was the eclectic Buontalenti, superintendent of public works and expert in all sorts of arts. He was asked to make various kinds of objects, including bowls and vases in semi-precious stones, and stage designs. He would even plan festivities and firework shows. In fact, Buontalenti was so famous for this that he was nicknamed "Bernardo delle girandole" ("Pinwheel Bernardo"). But this Grand Duke's intellectual masterpiece was the Uffizi, where he gathered the Medici collections and the octagonal Tribune designed by Buontalenti. Francesco also contributed to increasing the number of Medici villas. Special mention must be made of Villa Pratolino, built

by Buontlaneti and nestled in an immense park with grottos, fountains, and machines, including the towering giant *Apennine* by Giambologna.

By will of his father Cosimo, Pope Pious v elected him cardinal at the age of 14. But in 1587, when Francesco died, his brother **Ferdinando** i (Florence 1549–1609) gave up the title of cardinal in order to become Grand Duke. Ferdinando was a peaceful sovereign who was able to re-establish serenity and win back the trust of his contemporaries. Through a series of marriages, especially the one to Christina of Lorraine, he attempted to consolidate the power of the Medici family with some of the most important families in Europe.

He overturned former political alliances and strengthened ties with France while distancing himself from Spain. In 1588, Ferdinando founded the Galleria dei Lavori, later called the Opificio delle Pietre Dure, and commissioned the Forte Belvedere as well as the Villa Ambrogiana in Montelupo and the Villa of Artimino. He asked Giambologna to make the equestrian monument dedicated to Cosimo i, placed in Piazza della Signoria in 1594, and P. Tacca to execute a monument for himself for Piazza SS. Annunziata.

Cosimo ii (Florence 1590–1621) definitively put an end to the Medici family's banking activities. He appointed Galileo Galilei Professor of Mathematics in Florence. A learned and generous man, he was constantly ill. Cosimo died when he was just 31. He promoted the enlargement of Palazzo Pitti (entrusted to G. Parigi in 1618), whereas he asked his wife Maria Maddalena of Austria to re-build Villa di Poggio Imperiale (it was called this way because of its Hapsburg origins).

The Grand Duke introduced Florence to new types of painting that were in vogue in Europe during those years. He invited J. Callot and F. Napolitano to the city, and in 1620, he appointed J. Suttermans as the portraitist of the Medici. Before his untimely death, Cosimo II left a detailed will with precise instructions: he wished to entrust the regency to the Grand Duchesses, Christina of Lorraine and Maria Maddalena of Austria, respectively grandmother and mother of his son, who was the legitimate heir although still a minor. Hard times were in store for Florence: a sharp drop in trade, the Black Death that struck the city between 1630 and 1633, the effects of the 8 years of regency during which these two women wasted enormous amounts of public money.

When **Ferdinando** II (Florence 1610–1670) came into power, he was forced to deal with serious economic and health problems on the part of Florence's inhabitants. In the attempt to unite the Duchy of Urbino and the Grand Duchy of Tuscany, it was decided that Ferdinando would marry his cousin Vittoria della Rovere. But, despite the marriage, the union of these two states never actually took place because Pope Urban VIII was contrary.

A learned man who loved the arts, Ferdinando II contributed in a fundamental way to revitalizing the city's intellectual life. He promoted the Accademia del Disegno, the Accademia della Crusca, the Accademia degli Alterati, the Accademia degli Immobili, and the Accademia degli Infocati. In 1637, he refurbished the façade of the Church of Ognissanti and in 1640, he placed the equestrian monument to Ferdinando I in Piazza SS. Annunziata. He even commissioned G. da San Giovanni, F. Furini, C. Bravo, and O. Tannini with the decorations for the great hall of the summer apartments in Palazzo Pitti. His taste for the Roman Baroque art of P. da Cortona was rather innovative; in fact, this artist frescoed the winter apartments in Palazzo Pitti. Ferdinando received

many masterpieces from his wife Vittoria's dowry. Today, these can be found in Florence's museums. They include the *Portrait of the Dukes of Urbino* by Piero della Francesca, the *Venus of Urbino* by Titian, and various works by Raphael. He also collected clocks, chests, games, and objects made with semi-precious stones that he systematically chose with impeccable taste.

Grand Duke **Cosimo** III (Florence 1642–1723) was, unlike his prede-

cessors, a mediocre man who contributed (also because of his rather long reign, 1670–1723) to Florence's decline. Weak and a religious zealot, he installed a reign of terror during which Jews were persecuted (this was the only instance during the course of the entire Medici dynasty). Cosimo's only merit was that of having tried to resolve the Medici family's dynastic difficulties. Since his male sons had no children, he decided to destine the Grand Duchy to his daughter Maria Luisa. In this way, he aimed to ensure the autonomy of Tuscany. Nonetheless, it was only due to the decision reached by the great powers in Vienna in 1734 that Tuscany eventually passed into the hands of the Lorraine family. In the field of culture and the arts, Cosimo continued building the Chapel of Princes in S. Lorenzo, and his love for nature led him to collect still lifes. Among his most favorite artists: C. Dolci and the sculptor G. Zumbo, who created rather original, oftentimes macabre, works in wax. Ferdinando, Cosimo's first-born son who died at a young age in 1713, was a great admirer of art and enthusiast of Venetian painting. He purchased many works including the *Madonna del Baldacchino* by Raphael, the *Madonna delle Arpie* by A. del Sarto, and the *Madonna dal collo lungo* by Parmigianino.

Cosimo was succeeded by his son **Gian Gastone** (Florence 1671–1737). He is remembered as being rather lax in his habits and somewhat of a misanthrope. Nonetheless, he tried to remedy the persecutory laws his father had imposed. He commissioned a monument to Galileo that was then placed inside S. Croce.

Cosimo III's daughter, **Anna Maria Luis**a (Florence 1667–1743), was the last Medici to rule Tuscany. By marrying Giovanni Guglielmo, she was given the title of Electress Palatine. Anna was an intelligent and enlightened sovereign who carried out a generous act just a few years before she died in 1737: she donated the immense artistic patrimony the Medici had collected over the centuries to the Grand Duchy of Tuscany. Thanks also to her, the Medici have won an important place in history.

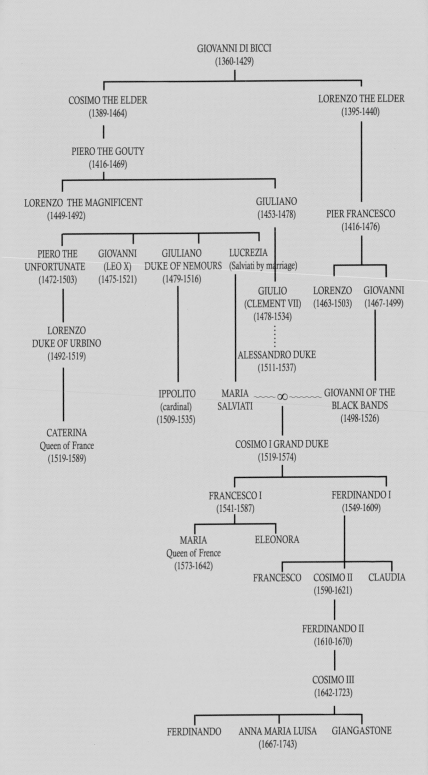

GIOVANNI DI BICCI
(1360-1429)

COSIMO THE ELDER
(1389-1464)

LORENZO THE ELDER
(1395-1440)

PIERO THE GOUTY
(1416-1469)

LORENZO THE MAGNIFICENT
(1449-1492)

GIULIANO
(1453-1478)

PIER FRANCESCO
(1416-1476)

PIERO THE
UNFORTUNATE
(1472-1503)

GIOVANNI
(LEO X)
(1475-1521)

GIULIANO
DUKE OF NEMOURS
(1479-1516)

LUCREZIA
(Salviati by marriage)

GIULIO
(CLEMENT VII)
(1478-1534)

LORENZO
(1463-1503)

GIOVANNI
(1467-1499)

LORENZO
DUKE OF URBINO
(1492-1519)

ALESSANDRO DUKE
(1511-1537)

IPPOLITO
(cardinal)
(1509-1535)

MARIA
SALVIATI

∞

GIOVANNI OF THE
BLACK BANDS
(1498-1526)

CATERINA
Queen of France
(1519-1589)

COSIMO I GRAND DUKE
(1519-1574)

FRANCESCO I
(1541-1587)

FERDINANDO I
(1549-1609)

MARIA
Queen of Frence
(1573-1642)

ELEONORA

FRANCESCO

COSIMO II
(1590-1621)

CLAUDIA

FERDINANDO II
(1610-1670)

COSIMO III
(1642-1723)

FERDINANDO

ANNA MARIA LUISA
(1667-1743)

GIANGASTONE

LIVING IN FLORENCE

Tuscan and Florentine cuisine

Tuscan, and especially Florentine, cuisine consists of simple and natural things that are typical of the farming tradition and closely linked with seasonal products. Every recipe, even though made up of few ingredients, is enhanced and embellished by the use of herbs and flavorings such as: garlic, onion, often with rosemary, sage and bay, but also spices, like nutmeg and pepper.

As a basis there is the best olive oil, slightly fruity and pungent, to be enjoyed raw. Then there's home-made bread strictly without salt (the origin of this practice arose in the 12th century, during the period of rivalry with the inhabitants of Pisa. They actually closed their doors to the Florentines for the sale of salt, who in response baked 'sciocco' or 'tasteless' bread, in other words without salt.)

Whereas 'schiacciata', salted focaccia with oil, is excellent with cold meats. Then there is the famous T-bone steak from 'chianina' cattle, which must be eaten thick, at least 5 cm, and cooked rare over embers. Then there are soups mainly of vegetables and pulses.

Today many Florentine restaurants offer traditional Tuscan dishes. We'll concentrate on the most common dishes to try, preferably in the typical 'buche', for an unforgettable underground experience.

Antipasti, side-dishes and snacks

CROSTINI TOSCANI - slices of bread spread with chicken liver pâté, anchovy and capers.

FINOCCHIÓNA - typical salami spiced with fennel seeds; the fresher variety called 'sbriciolona' is excellent.

FAGIOLI ALL'UCCELLETTO - a side-dish of stewed beans, fried in oil, garlic and sage with added tomatoes.

PANINO CON IL LAMPREDOTTO (🖐) – a very old Florentine sandwich made with the thickest and leanest part of a cow's stomach. It's cooked in a stock with flavorings and tomato. You can find it on the counters of the typical 'Trippai', to be eaten with a nice glass of 'Chianti'.

First courses

PANZANÈLLA - a summer country dish, made with stale Tuscan bread dressed with vinegar, fresh tomatoes and cucumber. The origin of this dish is ancient and strange; in fact it was used by farmworkers' wives as a way of sobering up their husbands. It's name is probably derived from 'zanella', a typical soup-bowl where the soaked bread was put.

PAPPA COL POMODORO - a soup made with stale bread and a tomato sauce left to boil into a broth. It's served hot with raw oil and basil.

RIBOLLÌTA (🖐) – a soup specialty made with beans, black cabbage (a typical cabbage variety that is grown only in Tuscany), stale bread and vegetables, cooked for a long time in a clay pot and later reheated. It gets its name from the custom of country women of cooking a large quantity of this soup that was 'ribollito', or reboiled, and eaten over several days.

Second courses

CIBRÈO - an old soup of rabbit and chicken offal mixed together with beaten egg.

INZIMÌNO - a sauce made of spinach or beetroot, garlic, parsley and tomato, which generally was used to dress calamari, ink-fish and dried salted cod.

PEPOSO DELLA FORNACINA - an old traditional dish of beef covered with red wine and pepper, cooked for many hours on a low heat in a clay pot. It's said that the inventor was Brunelleschi during construction of the dome

of the Duomo, who was concerned that the 'fornacini' employed to look after the fire during baking of the tiles, should have suitable food for their night-time vigil over the kilns. After the discovery of America, tomatoes and potatoes were also added.

ROSTICCIANA - tasty pork ribs spiced and cooked on a grill or over embers.

TRIPPA ALLA FIORENTINA - it's the stomach of a calf or a cow; it's eaten cooked in strips in a sauce of tomatoes, butter and lots of parmesan cheese. The summer variation is served cold, with pepper and fresh spring onions.

Desserts

CÉNCI - a sweet of very thin pastry, cut into strips and fried, typical of the Carnival period.

CANTUCCIO / CANTUCCÌNO - crunchy whole almond biscuits that you dunk in Vin Santo.

CASTAGNÀCCIO - a very flat autumn sweet made of chestnut flour, with pine seeds, raisins and rosemary.

PAN DI RAMERÌNO - a sweet leavened bread (that has been produced since the Middle Ages), with raisins and rosemary (called 'ramerìno') flavored with muscat grapes, typical of the Easter period.

SCHIACCIATA ALLA FIORENTINA - a flat rectangular dessert, typical of the Carnival period, flavored with oranges and coated with icing sugar.

SCHIACCIATA CON L'UVA - sweet bread pastry with grapes and rosemary, typical of the grape harvest period.

There is a vast selection of restaurants, but we recommend: *Buca Lapi* (Via del Trebbio, 1r) and *Trattoria Da Ginone* (Via dei Serragli, 35r), both run by local families. Whereas if you want to try something different, but traditional, we can recommend 'Cibreo Trattoria' (via de' Macci, 122r), 'Il Santo Bevitore' (Via S. Spirito 64/66r) and 'Il Cantinone' (Via S. Spirito 6r). You can enjoy a beautiful view and good food at 'Omero' (Via Pian de' Giullari, 11-Arcetri). If instead you want a good pizza, try 'Alfredo Pizzeria' (Viale Don Minzoni, 3r), the 'Semolina' (Piazza Ghiberti, 87r) or the 'O'Munaciello' (Via Maffia, 31r).

For sinful treats(!) try: traditional truffled sandwiches at *Procacci* (Via Tornabuoni, 64r), warm donuts (since 1943) at *Cucciolo* (Via del Corso, 25r), a great sandwich at *Fratellini* (Via de' Cimatori, 38r), ice cream at *Gelateria dei Neri* (Via dei Neri, 20r), and chocolate at *Hemingway* (Piazza Piattellina, 9r); the lean tripe sandwiches of *Orazio Mencioni* (Loggia del Porcellino). If you want to try a unique experience then you have to try the mega hamburger and the cheese-cake at *Ringo's Bar* (Borgo S. Jacopo, 19r).

For the nightlife there is a wide choice of fashionable places; however the *Café de Paris* (Piazza Dalmazia, 7r), the *Spleen Café* (Borgo S. Lorenzo, 31/r) and *Il Rifrullo* (Via San Niccolò, 53) are great spots.

PUBLIC EVENTS: FLORENTINE FESTIVALS

CAVALCADE AND FEAST OF THE WISE MEN (6 January) – of ancient tradition the feast takes place on the day of Epiphany with the parade of the Magi, followed by the Procession of the Florentine Republic in sumptuous costumes, following a route that goes from the Palazzo Pitti to the Duomo.

SCOPPIO DEL CARRO (Easter Sunday morning) - a feast with its origins in the countryside that goes back to the time of the crusades. On Easter Sunday the procession of the Historic Florentine Football

Game starts off from the Church of SS. Apostoli with the flints to be taken to the Duomo, that will be used to light the fuse for the explosion of the cart. About 9 meters high and affectionately called 'Brindellone' by the Florentines because of its uncertain gait, it hasn't changed since the 18th century; the mechanical dove starts off from there, following a line right into the cathedral, then returning to light the spectacular fireworks that are packed into the cart. Omens for the summer harvest were drawn from the successful outcome of the dove's flight.

La Fiorita (23 May) – an anniversary instituted in commemoration of the mysterious appearance of flowers and roses on the spot, in Piazza Signoria, where Girolamo Savonarola was burnt in 1498.

Patronal festival of St. John the Baptist (24 June) – in Roman times, the protector of the city was Mars; then, after the conversion of Florence to Christianity (between 500 and 800) John the Baptist was chosen, and was also stamped on one of the two sides of the florin as a guarantee of the coin's metal alloy (from which they still say today, 'St. John wants no cheating'). The celebration for the patron saint was carried out in the area dedicated to him between the Duomo and the Baptistery with a procession of the clergy and of men who carried candles, an offering that still persists today with a procession of personalities from the ranks of the citizens, the military, representatives of the districts and other authorities. As early as the 13th century the celebrations lasted several days, during which two competitions with very ancient traditions were disputed: one called 'Palio dei Cocchi', or chariot race, in Piazza S. Maria Novella, between 4 wooden chariots; the second 'Palio dei Berberi', 'The race of the Berbers', was a horse race that was run in the Ognissanti district. Today the palios have been replaced by the Historic Football match in Piazza S. Croce. At the end of the feast day, on the evening of the 24th June, fireworks are let off in Piazzale Michelangelo, an ancient spectacle that recalls the bonfires that were lit for the summer solstice in pagan days.

Historical Florentine Football (24th June and the Sundays before and after it) - also known as 'Football in Costume', it is a splendid event known throughout the world as a highly spectacular occasion that takes place in Piazza S. Croce. It's a traditional sporting competition of ancient origins played over 3 games, between 4 teams from the districts into which the city was divided, distinguished by colors (Blue for S. Croce, White for S. Spirito, Red for S. Maria Novella, and Green for S. Giovanni) and made up of 27 players each on a field covered with sand.

The purpose of the game, which is a mixture of football, rugby and all in wrestling, is to score "caccias", that is to say goals in the goal of the other team over 50 minutes to win the coveted prize of a white calf. The event is preceded by a procession of 550 figures of Historic Football that enters the field before the footballers, showing off magnificent 14th century costumes and making way for the display of the spectacular flag-wavers of the Uffizi.

Festa della Rificolona (7/8 September) – the festival started on 7 September with the peasants coming down into the city to sell their products in the market that was held in Piazza SS. Annunziata in honor of the birthday of the Madonna the following day. Anyone arriving in the depths of night would risk the walk with little lanterns of colored paper hung on a cane. Even today, during the night of 7/8 September, small groups of children can be

seen with those traditional multicolored and multi-shaped lanterns going around the city singing a typical nursery rhyme of the festival, ending up down at the river where the 'rificolone' are paraded in decorated barges. The origin from which the term 'rificolona', or rather 'fierucolone', is derived is curious, being a mocking term that the boys used to refer to the prosperous but roughly dressed country women who arrived in the city.

SHOPPING IN FLORENCE FROM THE PAST TO THE PRESENT

Florence is an attraction, not just for art, but also for shopping among the multiplicity of shops in the center. There is a vast selection of articles, from the most fashionable boutiques (the best streets are Via Tornabuoni and Via della Vigna Nuova) to the typical little Florentine craftwork shops, and then to the historical and traditional stores spread all over the city (if you like antiques the streets to go to are Via Maggio, Via dei Fossi and Borgo Ognissanti, whereas if you like the modern visit the famous Mercato delle Pulci, or flea market, in Piazza dei Ciompi). Whatever the case, it's worth pausing for a while and sitting at a table of one of the old cafés overlooking the Piazza della Repubblica, as the famous writers and artists of the 1800s and 1900s used to do, but be sure to check the displayed prices first.

Florentine craftsmen are renowned for the manufacture of clothing, shoes and leather accessories, although recently in many of the shops offering them for sale they are not 'hand-made', so you're advised to be careful before buying and not to be tempted by the 'special' prices so that you avoid any nasty surprises. Among the best is 'Parri's' (Via Guicciardini, 18r), a shop with more than 50 years' experience in the field.

If you like lace, embroidery and linen it's still not difficult to find those who are engaged in this art. In this regard we should mention TAF, 'Tovagliati Artistici Fiorentini' (Via Por S. Maria, 22r).

Gold and Silver occupy a special place in the Florentine tradition. The shops on the Ponte Vecchio are famous and there you can find wonderful jewelry in gold and silver, as well as cameos and corals of many colors. If you want to buy silver go to 'Brandimarte' (Via L. Ariosto, 11/Cr).

The ceramic and terracotta products of Montelupo Fiorentino, an area close to Florence, are also very beautiful. Among the many shops the best is 'Sbigoli' (Via S. Egidio, 4r).

The manufacture of silk products is also very important for the city, although now there aren't many craftshops left that specialize in the sale of ties and headscarves. A visit worth making though, is to the 'Antico Setificio Fiorentino' (via Bartolini, 4).

For wines and food products there are the historical 'Pegna' (via dello Studio, 8) and 'Zanobini' (Via S. Antonino, 47r).

If you like body care products the tradition of the 'Officina Profumo-Farmaceutica of Santa Maria Novella' (Via della Scala, 16) is world renowned.

In recent years the outlet trend has become increasingly common and today many are opening in Florence too, such as 'Raspini' (Via Calimaruzza, 17r). While outside Florence: 'Centro The Mall' (Via Europa, 8 - Leccio, Reggello) and the 'Barberino Designer Outlet McArthur Glen' (Via Meucci, 1 - Barberino del Mugello). Among the markets to visit are undoubtedly the market of the 'Porcellino' and the market of S. Lorenzo, where you can find souvenirs, but again take the greatest care about what you buy and check the prices.

Index of Sights

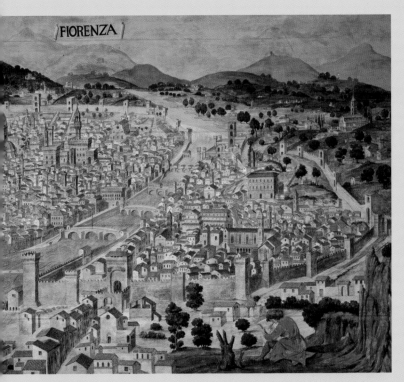

In 1252, the city minted its own gold coins, called *Florins*, with the image of the iris (the city's flower-symbol) on one side and *St. John the Baptist* (Florence's patron saint whose feast day is still celebrated on June 24) on the other.

As the economy thrived, the 7 Major Guilds, artisan corporations made up of bankers, wealthy merchants, and financiers of European rulers, began governing the city.

In 1293, the new nobility who had become rich as merchants obtained the "Ordinance of Justice" by excluding the prominent old aristocracy families from ruling the city.

But with the Hundred Years War, the crisis of Florentine banks (they had financed the insolvent King of England, Edward III), and the catastrophic outbreak of the Black Death in 1348, the lower classes slowly grew intolerant and revolted against those who belonged to the Major Guilds in the famous "Ciompi" uprising. Those who manufactured wool were able to form a Guild and take part in the government. But shortly afterwards, the new Guilds were abolished and power was reclaimed by a few prominent families. The city split in two: those who were loyal to the old oligarchy, which revolved around the Albizi family, and those of more modest means—devotees of the Medici family, who came from the Mugello area and were rich bankers.

The *Florentine Republic* gained access to the sea by capturing Pisa and Livorno. Cosimo the Elder de' Medici made the city into a Signoria in 1434, thereby paving the way for centuries of cultural and political splendor. Cosimo ruled from his palazzo on Via Larga (Palazzo Medici-Ric-

cardi), whereas Palazzo Vecchio, the seat of the magistracy, lost more and more importance.

It was his grandson, Lorenzo the Magnificent, who consolidated, during the second-half of the 15th century, Medici supremacy and prestige thanks to his brilliant political strategy in which he forged alliances with powerful families in Naples and Milan. However, his son Piero was exiled because he proved incapable of keeping the French troops of Charles VIII out of Florence (1494). The Florentines reacted to this invasion with uprisings, exhorted by the preaching of friar Savonarola (excommunicated for heresy and burned at the stake in Piazza della Signoria). The *Republic* was re-established until 1512, which was when the Magnificent's sons returned to the city: Giovanni (who became Pope Leo X) and Giuliano, though both were later forced to seek refuge in Rome (1527). Florence then reinstated the Republic and appointed the Duke of Urbino as the city's Captain. In the meantime, the Medici were gaining more and more power in Rome, and even Giuliano de' Medici's illegitimate son, Giulio, was elected Pope Clement VII. After the Sack of Rome in 1527, this new pope forged an alliance with Emperor Charles V to besiege Florence (1530). The city surrendered in 1532. Once the Medici returned, Florence was transformed into a Duchy with Alessandro I, and then into a *Grand Duchy* with Cosimo I (1569), the son of Giovanni of the Black Bands, who was able to subjugate Siena. With him and his successors, Francesco I and Ferdinando I, many important constructions were built and the city flourished both culturally and economically. This magnificence lasted until 1737 when the last representative of the family, Gian Gastone, died without an heir. As a result, Tuscany was assigned to Francesco Stefano of Lorraine, the husband of Maria Teresa, the Empress of Austria. Thus began a long period of close ties with the Hapsburg-Lorraines, and the city was ruled by a Regency Council until 1765. In that year, Grand Duke Pietro Leopoldo, Maria Teresa's second child, arrived in Florence and implemented important administrative, financial, and agricultural reforms. The French Revolution brought Tuscany under French control during the reign of Elisa Baciocchi, Napoleon's

sister. However, the Lorraines reclaimed power with Ferdinando III until 1860, the year in which the Grand Duchy was annexed to the Kingdom of Italy of King Vittorio Emanuele II of Savoy. As Italy's new capital (1865-1870), Florence underwent drastic urban changes: streets and palazzos were built at the expense of important historical landmarks, such as the ancient walls, and large industries were established. During World War II, Florence was plagued by clashes between partisans and German troops; it was heavily bombed and centuries-old sections were completely destroyed. However, Ponte Vecchio was spared. In fact, the bridge even survived the 1966 flooding of the Arno, and today it has become a symbol of the city.

Piazza della Repubblica, Column of Abundance, *on the site of the ancient Roman forum*

Castagna Tower

Tabernacle of S. Maria della Tromba (*Palazzo dell'Arte della Lana*)

Porta Romana, in the fourteenth century walls

B. Poccetti and helpers, Map of Livorno, *Palazzo Pitti, Room of Bona*

Florentine painter, Piazza della Signoria with the Martyrdom of Savonarola, *Museum of S. Marco*

O. Vannini, Lorenzo among the Artists, *detail, Palazzo Pitti, Museo degli Argenti*

1. DUOMO and ORSANMICHELE

PIAZZA DEL DUOMO AND PIAZZA DI S. GIOVANNI

As the city's religious center, you'll find 3 of Florence's most important monuments on these 2 connecting squares: the DUOMO, GIOTTO'S BELL TOWER, and the BAPTISTERY.

◇
1 BASILICA OF S. MARIA DEL FIORE OR DUOMO (✋)

The first thing that catches your eye is the size of this church. It's 153 meters long, 38 meters wide at the nave, and 90 meters at the transept. In fact, it can hold 30,000 people. This is indeed one of the largest cathedrals in the world!

The present-day basilica was built upon a pre-existing church dedicated to S. Reparata (4th-5th cent.). During the 1966 excavations, the ruins of this church were found in the front part of the nave (you can visit these from the crypt).

The church was started in 1296 by the architect **A. di Cambio**, who began constructing the Palazzo della Signoria at the same time. The basilica took about 140 years to complete (it was consecrated in 1436 by Pope Eugene IV), and famous architects like **Giotto** (1334-1337 ca.), **A. Pisano**, **F. Talenti**, and **L. Ghini** took turns supervising the work. The way the church looks today dates back to 1887 when the neo-Gothic marble façade was finally completed by the architect **E. De Fabris**.

For the FAÇADE, De Fabris was inspired by a drawing of A. di Cambio based upon the glorification of the Madonna. In fact, in the sec-

tion above the main doors you'll see a *Gallery of the Apostles* with a central aedicule representing the *Virgin and Child*.

In the tympanum are the bas-relief of the *Eternal Father* and busts of celebrated artists. In the tabernacles of the pilasters, you'll find images of clergy members who played an important role in building this cathedral. The bronze doors, portraying the *Stories of Mary*, are by A. Passaglia and G. Cassioli (late 19th cent.).

The INTERIOR, with its Gothic layout, is in the form of a Latin cross with 3 naves divided by pillars topped with arches. The multicolored marble floor is attributed to **B. d'Agnolo**.

In the area in front of the CHAPEL OF THE CROSS in the left tribune, there's a meridian that was used to study astronomy by many scholars of the age.

The INTERIOR FAÇADE has 3 round stained glass windows designed by Ghiberti. The *clock* with prophet heads by **P. Uccello** is quite curious (1443). Below you'll see a lunette with a *Crowned Mary* by **G. Gaddi** and the *Tomb of Bishop Antonino d'Orso* (1321).

In the RIGHT NAVE, observe the *bust of Filippo Brunelleschi* (1446) by **Buggiano**, the *bust of Giotto* (1490) by **B. da Maiano**, and the splendid Gothic *stoup* (14th cent.).

Duomo:

Buggiano, Bust of Brunelleschi

Interior of the dome

G. Vasari and F. Zuccari, Last Judgement, *detail*

The DOME INTERIOR was frescoed beginning in 1572 by **G. Vasari**, but F. Zuccari completed it in 1579 with scenes taken from the *Last Judgement*.

At the end of the 2 side naves you'll see the door that allows you to climb up to the DOME. It's a long way up a narrow flight of steps (463), but your efforts will be rewarded with the breathtaking view of the city.

The stained glass windows of the tambour were designed by Renaissance masters such as L. Ghiberti, P. Uccello, Donatello, and A. del Castagno.

At the CENTER OF THE OCTAGON you'll find the *marble chorus* and the *main altar* (1555), both by **B. Bandinelli** and **G. Bandini**; the wooden *crucifix* on the altar is by **B. da Maiano** (1497).

In the CENTRAL TRIBUNE, under the altar you'll see the bronze urn, made by L. Ghiberti (1430-1440), that contains the relics of St. Zenobius, Florence bishop.

The 3 tribunes around the transept are separated by 2 sacristies: the OLD SACRISTY (or the Sacristy of Canons) and the NEW SACRISTY (or the Sacristy of Masses). The 2 entrances are topped with glazed terracotta lunettes by **L. della Robbia** (1444 ca.) and respectively portray the *Ascension* and the *Resurrection*. In the LEFT NAVE (bay IV), observe the painting by **D. di Michelino** depicting *Dante with the City of Florence, Hell, Purgatory, and Paradise* (1465).

As you head towards the exit, you'll come across 2 other monochrome frescoes dedicated to 2 illustrious leaders, *Giovanni Acuto*, by **P. Uccello** (1436), and *Niccolò da Tolentino*, by **A. del Castagno**

(1456). You can also admire the bust of the organist *Antonio Squarcialupi* (1490) by **B. da Maiano**.

More recent works in the cathedral include *Arnolfo di Cambio* by **U. Cambi** (1843) and *Emilio De Fabris* by **V. Consani** (1887). In the LEFT NAVE, there's also a lovely aedicule dedicated to St. Zenobius.

D. di Michelino, Dante with the City of Florence, Hell, Purgatory, and Paradise

Sacristy of the Masses

The Cow of the Duomo

P. Uccello, Monument to Giovanni Acuto

☺ **THE COW OF THE DUOMO** (Via Ricasoli side)

There's an amusing story that is told about this cow head, positioned on the Cathedral wall in commemoration of the animals that were used during its construction. A popular story, says that it is actually the head of a bull, put there by one of the stone-masons working on the building. He was the lover of the wife of a baker who had his shop close by. Discovering the affair and consumed with jealousy the husband reported the couple to the court and they were forced to stop seeing each other. Then, out of revenge, the lover placed the head of the animal right in front of the bakery window to remind the baker that he was a cuckold.

DOME (*PANORAMIC VIEW)

The famous dome by **F. Brunelleschi**, whose tomb can be found in the crypt, is approximately 115 meters in height and 45 meters in diameter. It occupies the great octagonal tambour between the transepts.

It was begun in 1420 after Brunelleschi had won the competition announced 2 years earlier. His project was innovatory and consisted in using a double-shelled self-supporting ribbed structure and a wall structure made up of bricks arranged in a herringbone pattern so as to provide greater compactness and solidity.

The work continued until 1436, the year in which Brunelleschi also began designing the lantern that would complete the cupola. However, it was **Verrocchio**, in 1471, who finished the lantern by placing the gilt bronze sphere on top.

Lightening and thunderbolts!

During the course of the centuries thunderbolts were a real curse for the Duomo of Florence: in 1492 and 1699 the cone of the lantern was damaged; in 1495 and 1586 the lantern itself was damaged and pieces of it reached as far away as Borgo San Lorenzo; while in 1836 lightening struck the bell tower. The dome, which over time suffered the most damage was struck in 1578, 1776, 1816 and 1855.

Among the most powerful bolts of lightening to fall on the church, some have passed into folklore; there was the one on 17 January 1600 that caused the cross, Verrocchio's gilded copper ball and numerous pieces of marble to fall. Even today it is still possible to identify the exact point of impact on the pavement in the area behind the apse. On 13 June 1776 a thunderbolt caused serious damage to the lantern, that knocked down a niche which crushed ornamentations and friezes below, seriously compromising the dome as well with major cracks and breaks.

The introduction of electricity about midway through the 19th century was not, as had been hoped, able to resolve this age-old problem: lamp-posts were installed close to the Duomo to illuminate the piazza and the event was acclaimed with enthusiasm as the great in-

novation that it was but also because it was thought that the installation would be an excellent remedy for the prevention of lightening. The work took several years and included the installation of a lightening conductor too, something that scientists had however been thinking about for some time.

On the occasion of the inauguration of the World Fair, that took place in Florence in 1861, the Duomo was illuminated electrically for the first time and the risks associated with lightening seemed finally to have been resolved. But on 16 August 1879 a bolt of lightening struck the dome once again, causing the collapse of various pieces of marble, among them a piece of rib about 5 meters long, that caused serious damage to the entire architectural structure as it fell, including Baccio d'Agnolo's terrace.

Other similar occurrences, although of less severity, took place in the following years.

It was only in-depth research into the functioning of lightening conductors and other initiatives of a scientific nature, such as for example the installation of a device on Giotto's bell tower to measure the electricity in the air, that eliminated the risk that other lightening bolts might fall onto the Duomo.

② ⑤

☺ **DANTE'S STONE** (Piazza Duomo, 54)

Here the celebrated poet Dante remained for entire days admiring the building of the Cathedral, sitting on a large stone. There's an anecdote in connection with this habit of the poet's about his amazing memory, which tells of an acquaintance who passed by who asked him if he liked eggs. Dante replied that he did. A year later they met again at the same spot and the man asked the poet: 'With what?' and the vates, who wasn't taken by surprise, replied, 'With salt!'

2 BAPTISTERY

A fine example of 11th-century Romanesque architecture, its layout is octagonal and it has a diameter of 26 meters (ca.). Its roof is pyramid-shaped and topped by a lantern with columns; it is also covered in white and green marble. It was the city's cathedral until 1128 and is dedicated to St. John the Baptist. Many illustrious men of Florence, including Dante, were baptized here. The INTERIOR consists in a single room embellished with marble and Byzantine-style mosaics on the vault. The images represent the *Heavenly Hierarchies*, *Stories of the Genesis*, *Stories of Mary and Jesus*, *Stories of St. John the Baptist*, and the *Last Judgement*. The marble baptismal font (1371) attributed to the Pisan school is rather interesting. The *Tomb of the anti-Pope John XXIII* by **Donatello** and **Michelozzo** is also lovely. You'll be able to see the remains (walls and mosaic floor) of a Roman house through a grid on the floor.

The Baptistery has 3 BRONZE DOORS: the one to the south is by **A. Pisano** (1336) and is divided into 28 tiles with *Stories of St. John the Baptist* and the *Cardinal and Theological Virtues*. The other doors (1403-1452) are both by **Ghiberti**. The one on the north side, also called the "Cross Door," depicts 20 scenes from the *New Testament* and 8 tiles with the *Fathers of the Church* and the *Evangelists*.

Michelangelo defined the east door as the *Gate of Heaven*. Ghiberti used perspective for the 10 gilt bronze tiles obtained with the "schiacciato" technique (flattened relief). The bas-reliefs depict *Stories from the Old Testament* enclosed in a frame with 24 niches representing biblical figures and 24 heads of artists including Ghiberti's own self-portrait (he is bald and is the fourth from the top on the right side of the left panel).

◇
3 ARCHBISHOP'S PALACE (Piazza S. Giovanni, 3)

The palace dates from the 16th century, was modernized in 1895 when the piazza was enlarged, incorporates the CHURCH OF S. SALVATORE AL VESCOVO reconstructed in the 1700s on a pre-existing Romanesque building whose façade can be admired in the little piazza to the rear. Inside you'll see frescoes by G. D. Ferretti, M. Soderini and P. Anderlini.

◇
4 S. ZANOBI'S COLUMN (Piazza S. Giovanni)

Erected in 1384 where an elm had stood that, so the story goes, although dry, flowered miraculously on 26 January 429, on contact with the corpse of S. Zanobi, bishop of Florence, while it was being carried to the Duomo.

Venetian mosaicists, mosaics of the vault of the Battistero
The Gate 'of Heaven' (copy)

◇
5 GIOTTO'S BELL TOWER (✋)

To the right of the cathedral you'll find the Bell Tower (also called "Giotto's Bell Tower"). Giotto began working on this splendid structure in 1334. With its square-shaped base, it is over 84 meters in height. You can access it from the rear exit of the cathedral. It's another long flight up (414 steps), but the wonderful *VIEW OF THE CITY* from on top is well worth it. Giotto was able to finish the first part of the foundations with hexagonal tiles. However, the work was completed by **F. Talenti** in 1359. The iconography of the lower section illustrates scenes of *Planets, Virtues, Human Activities, Liberal Arts, Sacraments*.

◇ 6 MUSEUM OF THE OPERA DI S. MARIA DEL FIORE (Piazza del Duomo, 9)

Inaugurated in 1891, it gathers sculptures, drawings, and vestments that were once located in the Baptistery, the Duomo, and the Bell Tower. In the ROOM OF THE DUOMO'S ANCIENT FAÇADE, works gathered from the 1587 façade demolition are found here. These include works by **A. di Cambio**, **Donatello**, and **N. di Banco**.

The 2 BRUNELLESCHI ROOMS display wooden models of the dome, the artist's funerary mask, and tools used while building the cupola. In the display cases, you'll also see *Illuminated Antiphonaries* (1525), objects in gold, and liturgical vestments.

On the floor above you'll find **Michelangelo**'s *Pietà* (1553), a work the artist intended for his own funerary chapel in Rome. It was brought here in 1980. In the ROOM OF THE CHOIR, you can admire those by **L. della Robbia** and **Donatello** (he is also the artist of the *Penitent Magdalene*, a wooden statue, 1455). Next come the ROOM OF THE TILES OF GIOTTO'S BELL TOWER and the ALTAR ROOM where Ghiberti's tiles, once located on the Gate of Heaven, are displayed.

Museum of the Opera di S. Maria del Fiore:

Donatello, Penitent Magdalene

L. Ghiberti, *Stories of Joseph*

A. di Cambio, *Madonna with Blessing Child*

Michelangelo, Pietà

Donatello, Choir

L.della Robbia, Choir

☺ CANTO DEI BISCHERI (via dell'Oriuolo)

The corner of Piazza Duomo and Via dell'Oriuolo is famous because this is the origin of the adjective 'bìschero' which is typical of Florentine speech. The word's origin is strange; it is actually derived from the noble Florentine family, the Bischeri, the owners in the 1300s of numerous plots of land and houses in the area of the Duomo. When it was decided to build the cathedral, the Municipality asked to buy the family's properties, but they wouldn't accept the price offered, and tried to get a much more lucrative deal. Then however, a fire destroyed everything, and the family was forced to sell them at a cheap price. As a result the term came to mean a stupid or naïve person (you're a real bischero!)

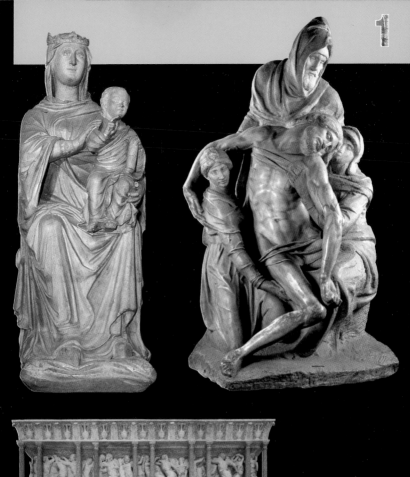

Air-raid Protection

During the course of the Second World War, because of the threat of aerial bombardment, steps were taken in Florence, as in many other Italian cities, aimed at safeguarding the most famous buildings and works of art, protecting them with special structures of wood and concrete.

Between December 1942 and February 1944 all the glass and windows of the cathedral were dismantled, the eyes of the dome armored, the fresco of Paolo Uccello removed, the Robbian lunettes bricked up and all the statues found both inside and outside the church were removed; in 1943 a plan was actually implemented for

The Galleria dell'Accademia with the protections installed during the Second World War to safeguard the works of Michelangelo.

a public air-raid shelter at the Duomo.

The bronze doors of the Baptistery were removed along with all the statues, and the Robbian lunettes were made safe while the bell tower was protected by a shell of reinforced concrete. Other defensive structures were provided for the *Loggia del Bigallo*, for the *Tabernacle of the Fonticine* in Via Nazionale and for the *New Sacristy*.

The horse and the statue of Cosimo I in Piazza Signoria were removed and many frescoes in the city's churches were protected with cushions.

The works of Michelangelo housed in the Galleria dell'Accademia were enclosed between special brick structures that during the war radically altered the appearance of the Tribune.

7 ARCICONFRATERNITA DELLA MISERI-CORDIA (Piazza Duomo, 19)

This ancient charitable institution, the Brotherhood of Mercy, founded in 1244 by S. Pietro Martire to help the sick and to bury the deceased, is headquartered in the 16th-century palazzo called of the 'Uffiziali dei Pupilli', and renovated in the 1700s. Inside you'll also find the museum containing paintings, prints and documents of this order that is still in operation in the Florentine area with thousands of members.

8 LOGGIA DEL BIGALLO (corner between Piazza Duomo and Via Calzaiuoli)

Of late Gothic style, this loggia was commissioned by the Compagnia della Misericordia to **A. Arnoldi**. Work was started in the mid-1300s. It was initially used as the Confraternity headquarters. Today, the **BIGALLO MUSEUM** is located here; it gathers works commissioned by the Bigallo Captains over the centuries (1300s-1700s), including the lovely *Madonna of Mercy* (1342). From here you'll see the most ancient section of Florence. The outside is covered in marble with reliefs representing biblical figures.

9 CHURCH OF ORSANMICHELE (access from Via Arte della Lana)

Located in front of the Church of S. Carlo, its name derives from the ancient oratory of S. Michele in Orto. This was replaced in 1290 by **A. di Cambio** to host the grain loggia-market. In 1380, the building became a church and the outside arcades were closed off. Tabernacles were then made to contain the bronze and marble statues of the patron saints of the various Guilds, commissioned to some of the city's most prominent artists (15th-17th cent.).

Church of Orsanmichele:
Donatello and Verrocchio, Tabernacle with Doubting Thomas
Orcagna and B. Daddi, Tabernacle with the Madonna of the Graces

Observe the splendid statues of *St. Matthew*, *St. Stephen*, and *St. John the Baptist* by **L. Ghiberti**; *St. George* (the original is found in the Bargello), *St. Peter*, and *St. Mark* by **Donatello**; *St. Lucy* by **Giambologna**; *St. Thomas* by **Verrocchio**; *Four Crowned Saints* by **N. di Banco**. Some of these statues are copies of the originals you can admire in the museum spaces recently opened to the public on the floors above the church.

The INTERIOR is rectangular, divided into 2 naves supported by pillars frescoed in the 1300s with images of the patron saints of the Minor Guilds and scenes from the Old and New Testaments.

At the end of the RIGHT NAVE there's the splendid *Tabernacle* by **A. Orcagna** (1355-1359); it is shaped like a baldachin and is embellished with gold and colored marble. At the center of the altar you'll see the altarpiece representing the *Madonna of the Graces* by **B. Daddi** (1347). Around the base there are scenes of the life and virtues of Mary, whereas on the back you'll find the artist's signature.

You'll find, on the north side, traces of when this place was used as a grain market: a weight and an outfall.

◇◇
10 PALAZZO DELL'ARTE DELLA LANA

Adjacent to Orsanmichele (actually, it's connected by a raised corridor), it was the 14th-century palazzo of the richest Major Guilds. It looks like a house-tower and today the offices of the Società Dantesca are located here, as can be seen by a fresco on the outside depicting the poet Dante.

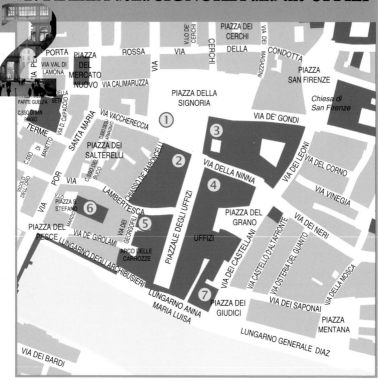

B. Ammannati, Neptune (il Biancone")

◇
1 PIAZZA DELLA SIGNORIA (✋)

This square is still considered the political center of the city.

On the left you'll find the *Equestrian Monument of Cosimo I* (1594) by the Flemish artist **Giambologna**; there's also a marble fountain (1575) by **B. Ammannati** portraying *Neptune* (also called "il Biancone") on a chariot drawn by sea horses with bronze satyrs and nymphs. A round granite plaque, located in front of the fountain, commemorates the site where the preacher Savonarola was burned at the stake in 1498. On the steps leading to Palazzo Vecchio you can admire, from left to right: the *Marzocco*, or a lion (in fact, a few real ones were kept at the back of the palace!). These animals were also one of the city's symbols. The original statue (1438) is by **Donatello** and can be found at the Bargello Museum. Next you'll find a recent bronze copy of *Judith and Holofernes* (1460), also by Donatello (the original is kept in the Fleur-de-Lis Hall inside the palazzo). There's also a marble copy of **Michelangelo**'s *David* (the original is on display at the Accademia Gallery). And finally, there's *Hercules and Cacus* by **B. Bandinelli** (1534).

24

Luigi Arrighetti, Copy of David

B. Bandinelli, Hercules and Caucus

Giambologna, The Rape of the Sabines

$\diamond$ 2 LOGGIA DEI LANZI

Also known as the "Loggia della Signoria," it was intended as a meeting point for public assemblies and ceremonies during the Signoria. The loggia was built by B. di Cione and S. Talenti between 1376 and 1382 and is based upon a drawing by A. Orcagna. After the fall of the Florentine Republic, the "Lanzichenecchi" (lansquenets) of Duke Alessandro I de' Medici occupied the loggia (that's how it got its derogatory name "dei Lanzi"). Cosimo I transformed the loggia's function from political to artistic and allowed it to become a place for artists and sculptors.

Late-Gothic in style, the loggia is decorated with lobed tiles with emblems of the Florentine Republic symbolizing the *theological and cardinal Virtues*. On the right in the first row, you'll find the lovely marble *Rape of the Sabines* (1583) and *Hercules and the Centaur* (1599), both by **Giambologna**. Next there's a Hellenic copy of *Menelaus Holding the Dead Body of Patroclus*, whereas the *Rape of Polissena* by **P. Fedi** is more recent (1866).

Under the left arch you'll see the splendid bronze *Perseus* (1554) by **B. Cellini** as he displays Medusa's slain head. The hero's bandoleer bears the artist's name and date. You'll also see 6 Roman statues of women against the back wall.

◇
3 PALAZZO VECCHIO

The **Palazzo dei Priori** (also known as Palazzo "Vecchio" or Palazzo della "Signoria"), with its parallelepiped-shape, is truly a splendid building.

Conceived in 1293 as a civil monument intended to host the Priors, **A. di Cambio** began working on the palace in 1299. In the 15th century, it passed to the Signoria, and was called "Vecchio" (old) when Cosimo I decided to move his residence from here to Palazzo Pitti (1565). Between 1865 and 1870 the Italian Parliament was located here when Florence was the nation's capital. Since 1872, the Municipality's administrative offices are found here.

The palace resembles a fortified structure with a majestic bell tower (1310) 94 meters high. Covered in rustic ashlar-work in *pietra forte*, it is divided into 3 levels, 2 of which have mullioned windows. On the top section you'll see a row of arches adorned with the 9 emblems of the Florentine Republic. There's also a landing shielded by Guelph merlons. The palazzo was enlarged over the years (starting in 1453). Michelozzo, Vasari (1558), and B. Buontalenti

(1588) all worked on the palace. Vasari is credited with the decorations in the FIRST COURTYARD with grotesque art and frescoes with views of cities of the Hapsburg Empire (1565) that were executed on the occasion of the wedding festivities of Francesco I de' Medici and Giovanna of Austria. At the center you'll find the *Putto with Dolphin* fountain (1476) by **Verrocchio**. You should then reach the COURTYARD OF CUSTOMS where you'll see a weather-vane with a lion and a lily, originally located on the top of the tower.

HALL OF THE FIVE HUNDRED - Take either grand staircase (made by Vasari). You'll reach the celebrated "Salone dei Cinquecento" designed by **Cronaca** in 1495. This room (53 meters long and 22 meters wide) was intended to meet the needs of the Republican government by hosting the General Council.

In 1563, it became a reception hall under Cosimo I, who had it frescoed by Vasari. The artist sought the help of various collaborators to decorate the walls and ceiling with scenes depicting the *Apotheosis of Cosimo I* and with allegories of the city's sections, of the provinces subjugated by the Grand Duke, of stories about Florence, of the episodes of war against Pisa and Siena.

HEARING HALL (north wall) - Located in a raised position with respect to the rest of the hall, it was intended for the Grand Duke's throne. In the niches, you'll see marble statues including those by **Bandinelli**: from the left *Cosimo I*, then *Giovanni of the Black Bands*, *Leo X*, and *Alessandro de' Medici*. On the wall opposite the entrance you'll find the *Genius of Victory* (1534) by **Michelangelo**, a work that was initially intended for the tomb of Pope Julius II.

STUDIOLO OF FRANCESCO I (door to the left of the entrance) - Decorated by Vasari (1572) and pupils, this was dedicated to Francesco's studies in science. The walls hide cabinets where the Prince jealously kept his collections and are adorned with the allegorical figures of *Prometheus*, the *Four Elements*, and man's activities. At the corners of the vault you'll see various human states of mind. In the lunette tondos, you'll find the portraits of *Eleanor of Toledo* and *Cosimo I* by **Bronzino**.

Palazzo Vecchio: first courtyard
Hall of the Five Hundred
Michelangelo, The Genius of Victory
Francesco I's Studiolo

The small statues in the niches represent mythological divinities.

The cabinets hide the *Tesoretto* (desk) Cosimo I commissioned in 1559 to contain his treasures (this was also decorated by Vasari with the symbols of the 4 Evangelists).

APARTMENTS OF LEO X (access from the Hall of the Five Hundred) - Composed of 6 rooms with Vasarian paintings (1562) that celebrate the Medici family.

The HALL dedicated to Leo X is frescoed with episodes from the life of Cardinal Giovanni, Lorenzo de' Medici's son who became pope in 1513, and marble busts portraying members of the Medici family. The other rooms cannot be visited in that they are administrative offices; these include the HALL OF CLEMENT VII (with the fresco *Siege of Florence of 1529-1530*), the HALL OF GIOVANNI OF THE BLACK BANDS, the HALL OF COSIMO I, the HALL OF LORENZO THE MAGNIFICENT, and the HALL OF COSIMO THE ELDER. Each of these rooms is decorated with portraits and scenes from the life of the person it is dedicated to.

APARTMENTS OF THE ELEMENTS (access from the Hall of Leo X) - Composed of 5 rooms designed by G.B. del Tasso (1550) and decorated by Vasari and his assistants. The first room, called the HALL OF ELEMENTS, is embellished with scenes that refer to the 4 primary elements, whereas the marble fireplace was designed by Ammannati. There's a spectacular view of the city from the LOGGIATO OF SATURN. (*PANORAMIC VIEW)

There are also the HALL OF HERCULES (with paintings of the *Labors of*

Chapel of Eleanor
Hearing Hall
Fleurs-de-Lis Hall

Hercules and an ebony cabinet with semi-precious stones), the HALL OF JOVE (with 16ᵗʰ-century Florentine tapestries and the original *Putto with Dolphin* statue by Verrocchio), and the HALL OF CERES (with 16ᵗʰ-century tapestries and paintings).

APARTMENTS OF ELEANOR OF TOLEDO (access from the landing that faces the Hall of the Five Hundred) - The ceiling of the GREEN HALL is decorated with grotesque art by **R. del Ghirlandaio**. Next you'll see the chapel with frescoes by **Bronzino**, who also painted the lovely altarpiece (1540-1545). Other rooms include the HALL OF THE SABINES, the HALL OF ESTHER (with a 15ᵗʰ-century marble lavabo and Florentine tapestries), the HALL OF PENELOPE, and the GUALDRADA ROOM (a bedroom dedicated to marital fidelity and decorated with scenes of games and festivities by the Flemish artist Jan Van der Straet).

CHAPEL OF THE PRIORS OR OF THE SIGNORIA - This chapel was built by **B. d'Agnolo** (1514) and was decorated by Ghirlandaio with biblical scenes.

HEARING HALL (from the marble doorway in the Chapel) - Created by **B. da Maiano**, here you can admire the gilded ceiling with octagonal coffers bearing the emblem of the Florentine people (by **G. da Maiano**, 1478).

FLEUR-DE-LIS HALL - This room stands out for its magnificent marble entrance by **G.** and **B. da Maiano** (1481) with inlaid panels representing Dante and Petrarch. The wood ceiling is decorated with gold lilies set against a sky-blue background (the lily was the symbol of the Anjou family). You'll also find here the original *Judith and Holofernes* (1460 ca.), **Donatello**'s masterpiece.

Other rooms include the GUARDAROBA (or storage room) or the HALL OF MAPS where the Medici stored their precious objects. If you head to the MEZZANINE, you'll reach the 3 rooms that host the *Loeser Collection* (seasonal opening), donated in 1928 to the Municipality by the American art critic Charles Loeser. It gathers Tuscan school paintings and sculptures (14ᵗʰ-16ᵗʰ cent.).

☺ **L'IMPORTUNO** (The 'Nuisance', on the right main entrance Palazzo Signoria, corner of piazzale degli Uffizi)

They say that this profile of a man was carved by Michelangelo, with a chisel and a mallet on an ashlar block with his hands behind his back while, interrupted for the umpteenth time at that spot, he listened to the words of a prattler.

Michelangelo (attr.),
"L'Importuno"

◇
4 THE UFFIZI (♨)

Right next to Palazzo Vecchio you'll find the Uffizi, commissioned to Vasari by Cosimo I de' Medici in 1560; he wanted to reunite the 13 city magistracies in a single location. Vasari decided to make the most of the area that extends towards the Arno. He demolished the buildings, including the Romanesque Church

A. Allori, The Marriage at Cana, *church of S. Agata*

Scenes from a Marriage

In 1540 Duke Cosimo abandoned his home in Via Larga and moved along with his court to the Palazzo della Signoria. Inside the palace, the room previously intended by Abbott Savonarola for the People's General Council, was transformed by Vasari some years later into a reception hall, decorated with an elaborate set of icons which has been reworked several times, and which is currently dominated by Leonardo's fresco of the *Battle of Anghiari*. During the course of the 16th century the room became the perfect place for organizing feasts, entertainments and official ceremonies commissioned by the princes.

Among the most celebrated of the banquets held in the Salone dei Cinquecento, was the one thrown in 1600 on the occasion of the marriage of Maria de' Medici with Henry iv, king of France. The direction of the event was entrusted to Bernardo Buontalenti who, in accordance with the Mannerist style of the time, wanted to inspire wonder among the guests by transforming reality into a scene of fantasy.

The hall was radically transformed: numerous mirrors were inserted into the set tables that were made to revolve by means of a special mechanism, so that the mirrors constantly reflected views of the feast; in this way the guests were able to admire the scene from a variety of angles and the ladies could adjust their make-up without having to leave the table.

The picture was completed by the imposing display of paintings produced by the greatest artists of the day active in Florence, which had as their theme the marriage of Maria itself: the principal participants of the event were thus able to admire themselves, not only in the mirrors, but also in the great painted canvasses, giving an additional and amazing double effect.

The food served at the marriage feast, which to a typically baroque taste must have seemed very different, and once again astonishing, was a resounding success. From the menu of the court's cooks we can read of 'boned ham in the form of a cockerel', 'veal pies in the shape of a boar' and 'gelatine bells with live fish inside', while the account of the marriage written by Michelangelo Buonarroti the Younger describes the splendid statues and sculptures in sugar conceived by Giambologna and Pietro Tacca depicting buildings, people and animals, as well as mythological scenes, cupids, monsters and also necklaces, clasps and jewels, displayed on a table with napkins, plates, cups and cutlery all made completely of sugar.

of S. Pier Scheraggio, that were there. The project consisted in 2 long, Doric-style porticos that went from Palazzo Vecchio to the Loggia della Signoria, joined by a splendid loggia in the section facing the Arno. (*PANORAMIC VIEW)

On the back arch you'll find the *Statue of Cosimo I* (1585) by **Giambologna**, whereas in the niches against the pillars you'll see statues of prominent Tuscans.

The work was completed in 1580 by A. Parigi and B. Buontalenti, who followed the desire of Francesco I (Cosimo I's successor) to make the Uffizi into a Gallery. A Tribune was created (1584) where the Grand Duke placed his most prized treasures. The offices were moved to other locations and the Gallery of Greek and Roman statues began to take shape. His successors enriched the collection with other sculptures, mathematical instruments, and scientific rarities. In the 1600s, Vittoria della Rovere's dowry consisted in an impressive quantity of works of art including many paintings by Raphael, Titian, and Piero della Francesca. More works, especially paintings, arrived with Cardinal Leopoldo, Cosimo II, and Pietro Leopoldo. The "Family Pact" (1737) between Anna Maria Luisa, the last Medici, and the Lorraine family was decisive in that she bound the entire Medici collection to the city of Florence with the obligation of making it accessible to the public.

ENTRANCE AND VESTIBULE - On the ground floor you'll see the remains of the Church of S. Pier Scheraggio and the frescoes of *Illustrious Men* (mid-1400s) by **A. del Castagno** (try to identify Dante, Petrarch, and Boccac-

cio). On the right wall you'll see the painting of **C. Cagli**, the *Battle of St. Martin* (1936). On the left, the *Annunciation* (1481) by **Botticelli**.

GABINETTO DEI DISEGNI E DELLE STAMPE - Located on the floor above, this room contains drawings and prints by Italian and foreign artists (15th-20th cent.). There are also originals by Leonardo, Raphael, and Michelangelo. Continue on to the next floor. You'll reach the corridors with ceilings that are adorned with grotesque art by 16th-century Florentine masters.

ROOM 1 - Gathers classical sculptures, mostly Roman. A copy of the *Doryphorus* by Polyclitus and the *Athlete* stand out.

ROOM 2 THE DUECENTO AND GIOTTO - This room resembles a medieval church. It displays lovely crucifixes and works by Tuscan school artists such as **Giotto** with his *Ognissanti*

Prospect of the Uffizi on Lungarno
Uffizi:
Doryphorus, *Roman copy*
A. del Castagno, Queen Tomiri
Leonardo, Woman's Head

Giotto, Madonna d'Ognissanti
Gallery Corridor
S. Martini and L. Memmi, Annunciation
G. da Fabriano, Adoration of the Magi

Majesty (1310 ca.) and the *Badia Polyptych* (1300 ca.); **Cimabue** with the *St. Trinita Majesty* (1280-1290 ca.); **D. di Buoninsegna** with his *Rucellai Madonna* (1285 ca.).

ROOM 3 THE SIENESE TRECENTO - Room dedicated to the pupils of Duccio and Giotto. On display are works by **S. Martini** and **L. Memmi** (the splendid gold *Annunciation* triptych, 1333), **A. Lorenzetti** (*Presentation at the Temple*, 1342, and the *Stories of St. Nicholas of Bari*, 1330 ca.), **P. Lorenzetti** (*Altarpiece of the Blessed Humility*, 1340 ca., and the *Madonna and Child Enthroned with Angels*, 1340?).

ROOM 4 THE FLORENTINE TRECENTO - This room gathers Giotto school paintings. These include *St. Cecilia and Stories of her Life* (1304 ca.) attributed to the **Master of the S. Cecilia**; the *Madonna Enthroned with Angels and Saints* (1355) by **T. Gaddi**; the *Madonna with Child and St. Matthew and St. Nicholas* (1328) and the *Polyptych of St. Pancras* by **B. Daddi**. There are also works by **N. di Cione** (*Crucifixion*, 1350 ca.) and **A. di Cione**, also known as **Orcagna** (*Triptych of St. Matthew*). But the painting that is most

similar to Giotto's style is the *Pietà* (second-half 14th cent.*)* by **Giottino**.

ROOMS 5-6 INTERNATIONAL GOTHIC - Rooms dedicated to Italian painters of the late 14th and early 15th centuries (this period is known as Late Gothic or "flowery" Gothic for the abundance of decoration). Here you'll see the *Crucifixion* by **A. Gaddi**, the son of Taddeo; the *Madonna with Child* by **J. Bellini**; the *Adoration of the Magi* (1423) and the *Four Saints from the Quaratesi Polyptych* by **G. da Fabriano**; the *Crowning of the Virgin* (1414) and the *Adoration of the Magi* (1420 ca.) by **L. Monaco.**

ROOM 7 EARLY RENAISSANCE - On display are important works by Tuscan painters (early 1400s). You'll see paintings by **P. della Francesca** (his famous *Diptych of the Dukes of Urbino*, 1472 ca., portraits of Federico da Montefeltro and his wife Battista Sforza; on the back there's the Flemish-style allegory of the *Dukes in Triumph*); **P. Uccello** (*Battle of St. Romano*, undated, was painted for the apartments of Cosimo the Elder); **Masaccio** (*Madonna with Child*); **Masaccio** and **Masolino** (*St. Anne Metterza*, 1424 ca.). Masaccio-inspired works include those by **B. Angelico** (*Crowning of the Virgin*, 1435 ca., and the *Madonna with Child*). Another masterpiece is the *Altarpiece of St. Lucy de' Magnoli* (1445 ca.) by **Veneziano**.

ROOM 8 LIPPI - This room is dedicated to the Carmelite monk and his pupils. You'll find Lippi's *Novitiate Altarpiece* (1445 ca.), the *Pala Barbadori* predella, the splendid *Crowning of the Virgin* (1447), the 2 *Adoration of the Child*, and the lovely *Madonna with Child and Two Angels* (1465 ca.) that inspired Botticelli. His pupils include his son **Filippino Lippi** with the *Adoration of the Magi* (1496) and *St. Jerome*, and **A. Baldovinetti** with the *Annunciation* and the *Madonna with Child and Saints.*

ROOM 9 POLLAIOLO - Here you'll find works by the brothers **A.** and **P. del Pollaiolo**. Look especially for the *Labors of Hercules* (1475 ca.) by Antonio; the *Portrait of Galeazzo Maria Sforza* (1471) and *Six Virtues* are by Piero and were intended to adorn the Tribunale di Mercatanzia. The *Fortress* was painted by Botticelli in 1470. Other works by this artist as a young man can also be found in this room

P. della Francesca, Diptych of the Dukes of Urbino

P. Uccello, Battle of St. Romano

Masaccio and Masolino, St. Anne Metterza

Filippino Lippi, Adoration of the Magi

Filippo Lippi, Madonna and Child with Two Angels

Botticelli, The Return of Judith to Betulia

Botticelli, The Birth of Venus *(the whole and detail)*

Botticelli, La Primavera *(the whole and detail)*

and include the *Story of Judith* series (1472 ca.).

ROOMS 10-14 BOTTICELLI - These rooms are dedicated to this legendary master. Here you'll see many of his works (1445-1510) and others by artists from late 15th-century Tuscan and Flemish schools.

Look especially for *St. Augustine in his Study*, the *Madonna of the Rose Garden*, and the *Portrait of a Youth with a Medal* (1475 ca.). In the early 1480s, **Botticelli** dedicated himself to "mythologies," or moral allegories that include *Pallas and the Centaur*, but especially the splendid *Primavera* and the *Birth of Venus*. You can also admire the *Madonna of the Magnificat*, the *Madonna of the Pomegranate* (1487) with its inlaid frame, the *St. Barnabus Altarpiece* (1487 ca.), the *Madonna in Glory with Cherubs* (1470 ca.), and *Calumny* (1495 ca.).

Leonardo, Adoration of the Magi;
Annunciation
Tribuna
Rosso Fiorentino, Musician Angel

In these same rooms, paintings by others can also be seen including the *Portinari Triptych* (1478 ca.) by the Flemish artist **H. van der Goes** and an *Adoration of the Magi* by **D. Ghirlandaio.**

ROOM 15 LEONARDO - This room is dedicated to **Leonardo** and to Tuscan and Umbrian painters of the late 1400s.

The legendary artist is present with his *Annunciation* (done while still a young man in around 1472) and the unfinished *Adoration of the Magi* (1481), which he started working on before leaving for Milan. In the *Baptism of Christ* (1475 ca.) of **A. del Verrocchio**, you can see Leonardo's touch in the figure of the angel on the left and in the background. There are also the *Crucifixion with Mary Magdalene* by **L. Signorelli**, the *Crucifixion with Saints* by **Perugino**, the *Adoration of the Shepherds* by **L. di Credi**, and the *Incarnation of Christ* (1505 ca.) by **P. di Cosimo**.

Rooms 16 to 24 constitute the museum's oldest corpus of works.

ROOM 16 MAP ROOM - The name of this room derives from the 3 geographical maps of Tuscany, frescoed in 1589 by **S. Buonsignori**. On the ceiling you'll also see 9 paintings by **J. Zucchi**.

ROOM 17 THE HERMAPHRODITE - Here you'll find the marble statue, a Roman copy, of the *Sleeping Hermaphrodite*.

45

P. di Cosimo, The Liberation of Andromeda

A. Mantegna, A Triptych from the Uffizi (The Ascension, The Adoration of the Magi, The Circumcision)

Giorgione and helpers, Moses' Trial by Fire

A. Dürer, Portrait of the Artist's Father Albrecht

Correggio, The Virgin Adoring the Child

Room 18 Tribuna - Created by Buontalenti, this octagon-shaped tribune was decorated by Poccetti and intended to gather the Medici family's most prized treasures. You can admire copies of classical statues like the *Medici Venus*, the *Young Apollo*, and the *Grinder* as well as 16th-century Florentine works like the celebrated Medici portraits of *Bartolomeo Panciatichi*, *Lucrezia Panciatichi*, *Maria de' Medici*, the young *Giovanni* and *Bia* by **Bronzino**, *Lorenzo the Magnificent* (1534) by **Vasari**, and *Cosimo the Elder* by **Pontormo**. Observe the splendid *Musician Angel* (1521) by **R. Fiorentino**, the *Madonna of the Well* (1518 ca.) by **Franciabigio**, *Lady with the "Petrarchino"* by **A. del Sarto**, and another *Portrait of Eleanor of Toledo with her Son Giovanni* by Bronzino (the dress she wears is the same one she is buried with). At the center of the room there's a table in semi-precious stones from the first-half of the 17th century.

Room 19 Luca Signorelli and Perugino - Here you'll find works like the *Madonna and Child* (1490 ca.) and the *Holy Family* by **Signorelli**, and the *Portrait of Francesco delle Opere* and *Monks* by **Perugino**, the *Annunciation* and the *Venus* by **L. di Credi**, the *Liberation of Andromeda* (1510 ca.) by **P. di Cosimo**, and the *Portrait of Evangelista Scappi* by **F. Francia**.

Room 20 Dürer - Works by German artists (1400s-1500s) are on display here. Look especially for the *Portrait of the Artist's Father* (1490), the *Adoration of the Magi* (1504), the *Madonna della Pera* (1526), *St. Philip* by **A. Dürer**; and the portraits of the *Prince Electors of Saxony* and *Luther*. Observe the ceiling with paintings on the *Views* of Florence.

Room 21 Giambellino and Giorgione - The works of Venetian painters can be seen here: **Giorgione** with his *Moses' Trial by Fire*, the *Judgement of Solomon*, and the portrait of the *Captain and Squire*; **Giambellino** and his *Sacred Allegory* and *Mourning*; **C. da Conegliano** with the *Madonna and Child*; **C. Tura** with *St. Dominic*.

Room 22 Flemish and German Renaissance Artists - Works by **A. Altdorfer** (*Stories of St. Florian*, 1530 ca.); **H. Holbein** (*Portrait of Sir Richard Southwell*, 1536, and a *Self-portrait*); **G. David** (*Adoration of the Magi*); **H. Memling** (*Portrait of Benedetto Portinari*, 1487); **J. van Cleve** (*Portraits of a Stranger and his Wife*).

Michelangelo, Doni Tondo

Titian, Venus of Urbino

Raphael, Self-portrait; Portrait of Leo x
with two cardinals

S. del Piombo, Death of Adonis

ROOM 23 MANTEGNA AND CORREGGIO - Works by **A. Mantegna,** like the *Madonna delle Cave* (1466), *Portrait of Cardinal Carlo de' Medici,* and the *Triptych,* and by **Correggio,** such as the *Madonna with Child in Glory* (1515) and the *Resting in Egypt* (1517 ca.).

ROOM 24 ILLUMINATIONS - Intended to house the collections of gems and semi-precious stones, it currently gathers the illuminations of Italian and foreign artists (15th-18th cent.).

In the SECOND and THIRD CORRIDOR, you'll find splendid Roman statues including *Cupid and Psyche,* the *Seated Nymph,* and *Leda.* (*PANORAMIC VIEW)

ROOM 25 MICHELANGELO AND FLORENTINE ARTISTS - Room dedicated to this legendary master and to other 16th-century Florentine artists. You'll see the lovely *Doni Tondo* (1506-1508 ca.) by **Michelangelo** with its original inlaid frame. You'll also see the *Annunciation* by **Fra' Bartolomeo** and the *Vision of St. Bernard* (1507), whereas the *Visitation* is by **M. Albertinelli** (1503).

ROOM 26 RAPHAEL AND ANDREA DEL SARTO - Many works by **Raphael** are located here: the famous *Madonna del Cardellino* (1506), his *Self-portrait,* the *Portraits of the Dukes of Urbino, Elisabetta Gonzaga,* and *Giudubaldo da Montefeltro,* and the portrait of *Leo X with Two Cardinals.* The *Madonna of the Harpies* (1517) and *St. James with Children* are by **A. del Sarto.**

ROOM 27 PONTORMO AND ROSSO FIORENTINO - Look for the *Supper at Emmaus* (1525), the *Portrait of Maria Salviati*, and the *Nativity of St. John the Baptist*. There are also paintings by **Bronzino**, Pontormo's pupil: the *Mourning* and the *Panciatichi Holy Family*. **Rosso Fiorentino** is also present especially with his *Portrait of a Girl*.

ROOM 28 TITIAN - Masterpieces by **Titian**, a master painter from the Veneto Region, are on display (his spectacular *Venus of Urbino*, 1538). Other works include *Flora* (1520 ca.), portraits of the Dukes of Urbino, *Eleonora Gonzaga*, and *Francesco Maria della Rovere*, *Portrait of Pope Sixtus IV*, the *Sick Man*, and the *Portrait of a Knight of Malta*. Here you'll also see works by **S. del Piombo,** Michelangelo's friend, like the *Portrait of a Woman* and the *Death of Adonis* (1511 ca.), and by **J. Palma il Vecchio,** also from the Veneto Region, such as *Judith* and the *Holy Family*.

ROOM 29 DOSSO AND PARMIGIANINO - This room is dedicated to **Parmigianino**, a mannerist painter and pupil of Correggio, and his *Madonna with Child and Saints* (1530), *Portrait of a Man*, and the *Madonna dal collo* *lungo* (unfinished work). You'll also see works by **D. Dossi** such as *Rest during the Flight into Egypt*, *Witchcraft*, and *Portrait of a Warrior*.

Room 30 Painters from Emilia - Look especially for the works of **L. Mazzolino** (*Madonna with Child and Saints*, 1522-1523) and **Garofalo** (*Annunciation*).

Room 31 Veronese - This room gathers works by **Veronese**, an artist from the Veneto Region active during the second-half of the 1500s: *Holy Family with St. Barbara and St. John the Baptist* (1564 ca.), *Annunciation*, *Martyrdom of St. Giustina*, *Esther Led to Ahasuerus*. There is also **Vicentino** with his *Visitation*.

Room 32 Bassano and Tintoretto - Works by **Tintoretto**: *Adam and Eve before God*, the *Samaritan at the Well*, and *Leda and the Swan* (1570 ca.). There are also the portraits of the *Venetian Admiral*, *Jacopo Sansovino*, and a *Man with a Red Beard*. In addition to this artist, there's **Bassano** with his *Two Dogs*.

Room 33 Hall of the Five Hundred - Works by Italian and foreign artists (late 1500s). These include paintings by **F. Clouet** (*Francis I of France on a Horse*, 1540 ca.), **A. Allori** (*Venus and Cupid*), **Vasari** (*Vulcan's Forge*), and **Bronzino** (*Allegory of Happiness*).

Room 34 16th-Century Lombard Artists - Works by **L. Lotto,** an artist who deals mainly with religious themes and is inspired by German artists (*Holy Family and Saints*, *Chastity of Susanna*, 1517, and *Portrait of a Youth*). There's also **G. Campi** and his *Portrait of his Father Galeazzo* and the *Portrait of a Musician*, along with **G. B. Moroni** and his *Portrait of a Learned Man* and *Portrait of Knight Pietro Secco Suardo*.

Room 35 Barocci and the Counter-Reformation - Works by **F. Barocci** like the *Madonna of the People* (1579), and by **Cigoli**, the *Deposition*. When Buontalenti's grand staircase was reopened, Rooms 36 to 40 were eliminated.

Room 41 Rubens - The paintings of **P.P. Rubens** are shown here and include *Henri IV at the Battle of Ivry*, *Henri IV Enters Paris* (1630), the *Bacchanal*, the *Self-portrait*, and the portrait of his first wife, *Isabella Brant*. You'll also admire works by his pupils: **A. van Dyck** with his *Equestrian Portrait of Charles V* and that of *Jean de Monfort* (1628 ca.). There

Veronese, The Holy Family with St Barbara and St John the Baptist

Tintoretto, Leda and the Swan

Parmigianino, Madonna dal collo lungo

Room of Niobe

is a famous portrait of *Galileo Galilei* (1635) by **J. Suttermans.**

ROOM 42 NIOBE - Sculptures portraying *Niobe* and *Niobides*. This statue, a Roman copy of an original Greek one (2nd-3rd cent. B.C.), was initially displayed in Rome, but later brought to the Uffizi in 1775. Pietro Leopoldo had a room built to house it. You'll also admire the lovely neo-Attic *Medici Vase* (1st cent.).

ROOM 43 THE ITALIAN AND EUROPEAN SEICENTO - Displayed are beautiful works by **A. Carracci**, such as his *Venus, Satyrs, and Cupids* and the *Self-portrait in Profile*.

ROOM 44 REMBRANDT - Works by the Dutch artist **Rembrandt** are shown here and include his two *Self-portraits* (1634 ca. and 1665 ca.) and the *Portrait of an Old Man*.

ROOM 45 THE ITALIAN AND EUROPE-
AN SETTECENTO - This room gathers
works by **G. M. Crespi** (*Cupid and
Psyche*), **P. Longhi** (*Confession*), and
by Vedutiste artists like **Canaletto**
(*View of the Doge's Palace in Venice*)
and **F. Guardi** (series of *Caprices*).
There are also many portraits in-
cluding the *Presumed Portrait of
Marie Adelaide of France Dressed
in Turkish Costume* (1753) by
J. E. Liotard, *Felicia Sartori* by the
Venetian artist **R. Carriera**, *Mar-
ia Teresa de Vallabriga on Horse* and
Maria Teresa, Countess of Chinchòn
by **F. Goya**.

ROOM OF CARAVAGGIO - Works
by Michelangelo Merisi, better
known as **Caravaggio**, the celebrated Milanese artist active in
Rome between 1593 and 1599, are
displayed here. You'll see his lovely *Bacchus*, the *Sacrifice of Isaac*, the
spectacular *Medusa* (which is actually a jousting shield that once belonged to Francesco I de' Medici). There's also *Judith Beheading
Holofernes* by **A. Gentileschi**.

Canaletto, View of the Doge's Palace in
Venice

F. Goya, Maria Teresa, Countess of
Chinchòn

A. Gentileschi, Judith Beheading Holofernes

Caravaggio, Bacchus; Sacrifice of Isaac

In the last rooms, you can admire works by B. Manfredi, G. delle Notti, and G. Reni.

There's a great view of the city from the terrace at the end of the corridor. (*PANORAMIC VIEW)

◇
5 ACCADEMIA DEI GEORGOFILI (Via Lambertesca)

Founded in 1753 and with Grand Duke Pietro Leopoldo of Lorraine as its patron, the academy, which has its headquarters in the Torre dei Pulci, is still noted today for its into agricultural scientific research and for its rich library (partially destroyed following a mafia attack in May 1993 that cost the lives of five people). Nearby you can find the 16th century PORTA DELLE SUPPLICHE conceived by **Buontalenti** with a split tympanum facing the outside and on top of which you can see the bust of Francesco I. The door was given this name because the people posted their supplications to the Grand Duke here.

◇
6 CHURCH AND MUSEO DIOCESANO OF S. STEFANO AL PONTE (Piazza S. Stefano)

The church, which today is a venue for classical music concerts, was mentioned in documents as far back as the 12th century. The lower part of the façade is Romanesque, with a marble portal, while the upper part is Gothic. Inside you'll find baroque-style works by Tuscan artists of the 1500-1600s; the *staircase* (1574) was designed by **Buontalenti** and the *marble altar* (1591) by **Giambologna**. The MUSEO DIOCESANO DI SANTO STEFANO AL PONTE has been set up next to the church, and there you can see paintings of sacred art and canonicals taken from deconsecrated churches. Among the works you'll find an *Enthroned Madonna*, an early work of **Giotto** and canvasses of P. Uccello.

◇
7 MUSEUM OF THE HISTORY OF SCIENCE (Piazza dei Giudici, 1)

Founded in 1927, this museum gathers over 5,000 scientific objects that once belonged to the Medici (the oldest ones date back to Cosimo the Elder) and Lorraine families.

The 2 floors are respectively divided into 11 and 10 rooms. In the exposition areas, you'll find Italian and foreign mathematical instruments (10th-19th cent.), including an Arabian *celestial globe* (1080) and the *armillary sphere* of Antonio Santucci (second-half 1500s). In Rooms 4-5, there are instruments that once belonged to **Galileo Galilei**, like his *objective lens*, with which this great scientist was the first to observe the satellites of Jove, his compass, and telescope. On the floor above you'll find instruments from the 18th-19th centuries.

The *mechanical paradox* is famous. Moreover, you'll see weights and alembics as well as Grand Duke Pietro Leopoldo's work desk and chemical compounds.

Buontalenti, Porta delle suppliche
Giotto, Enthroned Madonna, *Diocesan Museum of S. Stefano al Ponte*

3. PONTE VECCHIO and PALAZZO PITTI

◇
1 VASARI'S CORRIDOR (reservation required)

When the Uffizi was refurbished and enlarged, the Grand Duke asked Vasari to also make a secret passageway that would connect Palazzo Vecchio with the new Grand-Ducal residence, Palazzo Pitti.

This corridor, which was named after its architect (1565), begins inside Palazzo Vecchio, crosses the Uffizi Gallery, continues on top of Ponte Vecchio, and finally finishes, after about 1 kilometer, in the Boboli Garden where Buontalenti's grotto is found.

In 1973, the corridor was converted into an exposition space that today houses about 800 works. The vast *Collection of Self-portraits* of Italian and foreign artists begins in the second stretch (from Ponte Vecchio) and displays works from the 14th century to modern times. Look for the self-portraits of Vasari (1550), Del Sarto, Raphael, Titian, Bernini, Rosa, Canova, Reni, Rubens, Rembrandt, Velázquez, Liotard, Böcklin, Hayez, Fattori, Michetti, Balla, and Chagall.

As you walk unobserved along the corridor above Ponte Vecchio and cross the tribune of the church of S. Felicita, you'll enjoy some marvelous vistas of the city and the hills. (*PANORAMIC VIEW)

◇
2 PONTE VECCHIO (♥)

Made up of 3 solid arches, this is the only bridge that has survived since 1345, when it was rebuilt by Neri di Fioravante after the Arno had flooded. Moreover, it is the only bridge that escaped German bombings in 1944. In the late 1500s, Ferdinando I had the shops of the "beccai,"

Final stretch of Vasari's Corridor

Florentine butchers, replaced with goldsmith shops that still today occupy both of its sides. These shops even preserve their original, traditional wooden shop shutters. In one of the 2 terraces, you'll find the *Bust of Benvenuto Cellini*, a 20th-century work. (*PANORAMIC VIEW)

☺ **THE SUNDIAL** (Ponte Vecchio)

> *On a building at the corner with the terrazzo of the PONTE VECCHIO you can see a sundial from 1345 in white marble which is still useable and that, as pointed out on the plaque beneath, was positioned there to commemorate the flood that destroyed the bridge in 1333. The instrument, in the form of a goblet, faces south, which is also indicated by the sculptured lizard.*

◇
3 CHURCH OF S. FELICITA (Piazza di S. Felicita)

The church rests upon the foundations of a Paleochristian construction (4th cent.). It is considered the city's oldest sacred construction, even though it was rebuilt in the 1700s. Vasari's Corridor passes above the entrance portico. Inside, to the right you'll see the *Capponi Chapel*, which might have been designed by Brunelleschi in the early 15th century. Here, you can admire Pontormo's *Deposition* and fresco of the *Annunciation*.

◇
4 PALAZZO PITTI (✋)

In the 1400s, Luca Pitti wanted this palace to be built on the Boboli hill so as to challenge the power of the Medici. Designed in 1445 by Brunel-

leschi, this building initially consisted in a massive ashlar structure with 3 stories (including the 7 central windows) separated by long balconies.

After Pitti died (1473) and his family began to lose power, the palazzo was purchased by Cosimo I for his wife Eleanor of Toledo who moved the court here (1549).

B. Ammannati's first interventions did not greatly alter the façade; instead, the 2 side doors were closed off and replaced with "kneeling" windows, while the palazzo's surface grew in depth. Between 1618 and 1640, 4 more windows were added on each side of the façade by G. and A. Parigi and the interior was embellished. When the Lorraines came to power, G. Ruggeri and P. Poccianti were asked to continue working on this princely residence. Today, it measures 205 meters in length with 2 porticoed side wings called *rotaries*.

Under French domination (1799-1814) the palazzo became the residence of Maria Luisa of Bourbon, Queen of Etruria, and then of Elisa Bonaparte, who had the rooms in the left wing refurbished. In fact, during those years, the artists G. Cacialli and P. Benvenuti set up rooms in Tuscan neo-classical style, like the Bath of Napoleon, though it was never used by the Emperor.

When Florence was Italy's capital (1865-1870) King Vittorio Emanuele also lived here.

Today, 7 art collections are housed inside Palazzo Pitti.

From the central arch-shaped entrance you'll reach Ammannati's courtyard; he also executed the fountain situated above on the terrace, though

Moses Grotto

substituted in 1641 by the famous *Artichoke Fountain* by **F. Susini** and **F. del Tadda**. Below you'll see *Moses' Grotto*, a 17th-century work in porphyry. Lovely Roman statues are located under the portico; to the right you'll find the PALATINE CHAPEL with its mosaic altar and crucifix by Giambologna.

Take the grand staircase. You'll reach the PALATINE GALLERY and the ROYAL APARTMENTS.

PALATINE GALLERY

This collection gathers Italian and European paintings and masterpieces (1400s-1700s). Spread out in various halls, it was begun by Cosimo II in 1620 and later enlarged by Cosimo III. Thanks to the Lorraines, it was opened to the public in 1828. The museum itinerary follows the criterion of private "picture galleries," and therefore the halls are "decorated" by the paintings on display.

HALL OF STATUES OR OF CASTAGNOLI - Named after the artist who painted the room. At the center you'll find the *Table of the Muses* with inlaid semi-precious stones and a bronze stand by G. Dupré (1851).

Next you'll reach the HALL OF ALLEGORIES OR OF "VOLTERRANO": on display are works by **Volterrano (***The Practical Joke of Father Arlotto***)**, **G. da S. Giovanni** (*Venus Combing Cupid*), and **Suttermans** (Medici portraits).

Then you'll find other halls that have been converted, in more recent times, into exposition spaces (HALL OF FINE ARTS, OF HERCULES, OF AURORA, OF BERENICE). These gather works (mainly 17th-century altarpieces) taken from churches and convents that were suppressed during the 1800s. Next comes the HALL OF PSYCHE dedicated to the works of the Neapolitan artist **S. Rosa** painted during his stay in Florence (1640-1649), especially the *Forest of the Philosophers* and the *Battle*.

Stroll through the rooms set up for Empress Maria Luisa of Bourbon and you'll reach the HALL OF FAME with its Dutch-Flemish works like *Brushwood with Animals* by **O. van Schrieck** and the *Views* by **G. van Wittel**.

Heading back from the HALL OF FINE ARTS you'll come to the HALL OF THE ARK with frescoes by L. Ademollo. This room is pavilion-shaped like the one people thought housed the Ark of the Covenant.

MUSIC ROOM - Also called the "drum" room for the shape of the small furnishings it contains, you'll find a lovely table with a malachite top and stand in gilded bronze.

POCCETTI CORRIDOR - Frescoed by Rosselli, it contains small 17th-century paintings like *Ila and the Nymphs* by **F. Furini**, the *Martyrdom of St. Bartholomew* by **J. Ribera**, the *Three Boys in the Furnace* by **M. Rosselli**. There are also valuable pieces of furniture like the semi-precious stone table designed by **G.B. Foggini (**1716).

HALL OF PROMETHEUS - On display is the *Madonna with Child and Scenes from the Life of St. Anne* by **Filippo Lippi**, the Gallery's oldest painting (1450). You'll also find two panels by **Pontormo,** the *Adoration of the Magi* (1523) and the *Martyrdom of St. Maurice and the Theban Legion*, as

Volterrano, The Practical Joke of Father Arlotto

Filippo Lippi, Bartolini Tondo

Music Room

well as the *Holy Family with St. Catherine* by **L. Signorelli**. An 1844 Sèvres vase signed by L.P. Schilt is located at the center of the room. Cross the CORRIDOR OF COLUMNS where small-format Dutch and Flemish works (17th-18th cent.) are housed.

HALL OF JUSTICE - Gathers mainly 16th-century works from Venice and the Veneto Region. These include: *Portrait of Tommaso Mosti (?)* by **Titian**, *Portrait of a Gentleman* by **Veronese**, and the *Madonna with St. Catherine and St. John* attributed to **P. Lanciani**.

HALL OF FLORA - Here you'll find 16th-century Florentine works including the *Holy Family with St. Anne and St. John* by **Vasari** and the *Madonna with Child* by **A. Allori**.

HALL OF THE PUTTI - On display are paintings by Flemish and Dutch artists such as *The Three Graces* by **Rubens** and two *Still Lifes with Fruit and Flowers* by **R. Ruysch** (1715 and 1716).

HALL OF ULYSSES - Frescoed to celebrate Ferdinando III of Lorraine's return to Florence in 1815, it gathers important works such as the *Madonna dell'Impannata* (1514) by **Raphael**, the *Madonna with Child and Saints* (also called "Gambassi Altarpiece," 1525-1526) by **A. del Sarto**, and the *Ecce homo* by **Cigoli** (1607).

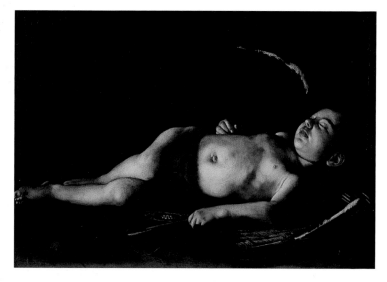

Pontormo, Adoration of the Magi
Caravaggio, Sleeping Cupid
Titian, Portrait of Tommaso Mosti (?)
Rubens, The Three Graces
R. Ruysch, Still Life With Flowers And Fruit
Raphael, Madonna dell'Impannata
A. del Sarto, Madonna with Child and Saints

Raphael: Madonna della Seggiola;
Madonna of the Grand Duke; La Velata

The Hall of Saturn

Giorgione, The Three Ages of Man

NAPOLEON'S BATH - Created in 1813 as Napoleon's imperial apartments, this space is frescoed and decorated with bas-reliefs.

HALL OF JUPITER'S EDUCATION - Originally the Grand Duke's bedroom, it houses the *Sleeping Cupid* (1608) by **Caravaggio**, *Judith with Holofernes' Head* by **C. Allori**, and *St. Andrew before the Cross* by **C. Dolci**.

HALL WITH STOVE - This hall, which got its name from the warm air that was used to heat it, was frescoed with allegorical paintings by P. da Cortona and M. Rosselli. Majolicas adorn the floor.

HALL OF THE ILIAD - Named after its frescoes with images taken from Homeric episodes. It contains works by Raphael, *La Gravida*; **R. Ghirlandaio**, *Portrait of a Lady* (1509); **A. del Sarto,** the *Passerini Altarpiece* and the *Assunta Panciatichi*; **Suttermans**, *Portrait of Valdemaro Cristiano*. You'll also find two paintings by **A. Gentileschi,** *Judith* and *Magdalene* (1614-1620).

HALL OF SATURN - Frescoed by Ferri, this room contains the most substantial core of Raphael's paintings, including the *Madonna della Seggiola*, the *Portraits of Agnolo* and *Maddalena Doni* (1507), the *Madonna of the Grand Duke* (1506), the *Portrait of Tommaso Inghirami*, and the *Madonna del Baldacchino*, which is unfinished because the painter moved to Rome. You'll also see *The Disputa on the Trinity* and the *Annunciation* by **A. del Sarto**, the *Lamentation over the Dead Christ* (1495) by **Perugino**, and *Christ as "Salvator Mundi"* (1516) by **Fra' Bartolomeo**.

HALL OF JOVE - This was originally the throne room, but today it contains the *Holy Family* by **Guercino**, the *Three Ages of Man*, recently attributed to **Giorgione** (1500 ca.), the *Madonna del Sacco* by **Perugino**, the *Pietà* by **Fra' Bartolomeo**, and the *Annunciation* by **A. del Sarto**. But the most celebrated work displayed here is *La Velata* by **Raphael** (1516), made during his stay in Rome; perhaps this work portrays the Fornarina, a woman the artist greatly loved.

HALL OF MARS - It contains mainly portraits from the Veneto Region

Titian, The Concert
A. Canova, Italic Venus
Throne Room

and a few Flemish and Spanish masterpieces. Among the works from Veneto: **Titian**, the *Portrait of Ippolito de' Medici*; **Tintoretto**, the *Portrait of Alvise Cornaro* (1560-1565); **Veronese,** the *Portrait of a Gentleman in a Fur*. Among the Flemish works: *The Effects of War* (1638) and *The Four Philosophers* by **Rubens** and the *Portrait of Cardinal Bentivoglio* by **Van Dyck**. The Spanish are represented by **Murillo** and his two paintings depicting the *Madonna with Child*.

HALL OF APOLLO - The altarpiece *Sacred Conversation* (1522) by **D. Mazza** dominates the room. You'll also find **Titian** with his *Man with Gray Eyes* or *The Englishman* and *Magdalene*. Other artists from the same Region are also present: **Tintoretto** with the *Portrait of Vincenzo Zeno* and **D. Dossi** with the *Nymph and Satyr*. There are also works by **G. Reni** (*Cleopatra*), Guercino, and C. Allori. You'll also see Flemish paitings by **Rubens** with his *Portrait of Isabella Clara Eugenia* (1625), **J. Suttermans** with the *Portrait of Grand Duchess Vittoria della Rovere* (1640 ca.), and **Van Dyck** with the *Portrait of Charles I of England and Henrietta of France*.

HALL OF VENUS - Frescoed with mythological scenes by **P. da Cortona** and **C. Ferri**. It displays works by **Titian** like *The Concert*, the *Portrait of Pietro Aretino*, the *Portrait of a Lady*, the *Portrait of Pope Julius II*; **Rubens** with his *Return of the Peasants from the Fields* and *Ulysses Landing on the Island of the Phaeacians*; **S. Rosa** with his *Seascape at*

3

Sunset and the *Seascape with Ships and Galleys*; **Guercino** and his *Apollo and Marsia*; **Cigoli** with his *Jesus Appears to Peter for the Third Time*. At the center of the room you'll find **A. Canova**'s marble statue *Italic Venus*.

ROYAL APARTMENTS

Located in the right wing of the palazzo, you can reach this area through the Hall of Niches. This was once the residence of the Medici and Lorraine families. The Savoy family also lived here when Florence was the capital of Italy (1865-1870). In fact, they left most of the furnishings we see today, including lavish tapestries and pieces of furniture. These rooms have been recently re-arranged and are divided into 14 areas.

HALL OF NICHES - The Medici used this hall as a waiting room for visitors. Under the Lorraines, it became a room for festivities and then a dining hall. Here you'll find niches with copies of ancient statues and Japanese vases.

GREEN HALL - Named after the color of the silk that lavishly covers the room, it was also called the "Guards' Chamber" because Prince Ferdinando's apartments were located nearby. You can admire a lovely painting by **L. Giordano** with the *Allegory of Peace between Florentines and Fiesolani* and the *Portrait of Fra' Marcantonio Martelli* by **Caravaggio**. This room is sumptuously embellished and also displays a small table with inlaid semi-precious stones and an ebony cabinet (1685 ca.).

THRONE ROOM - Or the "Red" room, it contains a throne, a baldachin, and a balustrade that were placed here at the time of the Savoy family.

It was used as a hearing hall under the Medici and the Lorraines. It contains Japanese and Chinese vases (18th-19th cent.).

SKY-BLUE HALL - The silk wall coverings in this hall are sky-blue in color. It was also known as the "Hall of Cymbals" because Grand Prince Ferdinando held concerts here. This stunning room is embellished with stuccos and Gobelins tapestries. You'll also find the 10 portraits of the Medici executed by J. Suttermans (1621-1645).

CHAPEL - Under the Medici it served as a bedroom; in the 1700s, it became a chapel. Note the *prie-dieu*, the altar with an ivory crucifix, and paintings by Titian, Rembrandt, and Van Dyck. **C. Dolci** is credited with the *Madonna and Child* with its lovely frame in tortoise-shell and semi-precious stones.

HALL OF PARROTS - This magnificent room has birds embroidered on the green wall coverings. It separates the rooms of the King and Queen of Savoy. The French clock in gilded chiseled bronze with a black marble base deserves special attention.

YELLOW HALL, QUEEN'S CHAMBERS, OVAL STUDY, AND ROUND STUDY - These were once Queen Margherita of Savoy's apartments, richly adorned with Gobelins tapestries and portraits such as the *Electress Palatine* attributed to **J.F. Douven**. Here you'll find a lovely cabinet in ebony, ivory, alabaster, and gilded bronze, a stoup, and other precious objects.

If you head back to the Hall of Parrots, you'll reach the apartments of King Umberto I of Savoy. This part is composed of the KING'S ROOM, the STUDY, the RED HALL, and the ANTI-CHAMBER. Characterized by furnishings that are less ornate than those found in the other rooms, you'll also find here tapes-

Queen's Chambers
Modern Art Gallery, *Hall of Portraits from the Age of King Umberto I*
P. Tenerani, Psyche Abandoned

tries, furnishings of the Lorraines, mirrors, a marble bust of the King, portraits by Suttermans.

APARTMENT OF TAPESTRIES - If you go through the HALL OF BONA (it was decorated by **B. Poccetti** in 1609 with the *Defeat of the City of Bona*), you'll reach the tapestry room. Composed of 5 rooms set aside for the ladies-in-waiting of the Medici court, it was later used to welcome illustrious guests. Each room was frescoed with personifications of the *Virtues* by the greatest artists during the time of the Medici. Splendid tapestries (French and Tuscan manufacture) depicting allegorical figures hang on the walls. The last hall, the WHITE ROOM, is decorated with stuccos that brighten up the room.

MODERN ART GALLERY

In the rooms that were once divided into the Chambers of the Arch Duchesses and the New Chamber under the Medici and the Lorraines, you'll find many noteworthy Italian paintings and sculptures (18th-20th cent.) in addition to some modern masterpieces by foreign artists. The collection was started by Grand Duke Piet-

A. *Canova*, Calliope

A. *Puccinelli*, Portrait of the Noblewoman
Morrocchi

F. *Hayez*, The Two Foscari

S. *De Tivoli*, A Pasture

A. *Scheffer*, Portrait of Princess Mathilde
Bonaparte Demidoff

G. *Fattori*, Self Portrait

ro Leopoldo in 1784 and continued under the Savoy family.

Over 2,000 works are arranged in chronological order and divided according to subject matter. The museum is comprised of 30 rooms.

The first ROOMS (1–2) are dedicated to neoclassical art and to French occupation in Tuscany. Artists include: **A. Canova** (bust of *Calliope*), F. Carradori, S. Ricci, **P. Batoni** (*Hercules at the Crossroads*), **P. Tenerani** (*Abandoned Psyche*).

In the following ROOMS (3–4), you'll find paintings dedicated to the iconography of Tuscan dynasties before the unification of Italy, like the Hapsburg-Lorraines and the Bourbons of Lucca (**F.X. Fabre,** the *Portrait of Maria Luisa of Bourbon, Queen of Etruria*), and of the families that contributed in a significant way to Florence, like the Demidoff family (the *Portrait of Princess Matilde Bonaparte Demidoff* by **A. Scheffer**).

ROOMS 5 and 6 display historical romantic art and ideal landscapes. You'll find works by **F. Hayez** (*The Two Foscari*), **G. Sabatelli** (*Giotto and Cimabue*), and **M. d'Azeglio** (*Attack of the Cavalry*).

Among the sculptures that can be found here: **P. Fedi** (*St. Sebastian*) and **G. Dupré** (*Little Bacchus of the Cryptogam*).

ROOMS 7 and 8 contain commemorative portraits and portraits from when Florence was the capital of Italy. These include: **A. Ciseri** (*Giovanni Dupré*), **R. Sorbi** (*Portrait of the Sculptor Emilio Zocchi*), **A. Puccinelli** (*Portrait of the Noblewoman Morrocchi*), **G. Fattori** (*Self-portrait*).

ROOM 9 is dedicated to landscape artists from the mid-1800s. Works include: **A. Fontanesi** (*After the Rain*) and **S. De Tivoli** (*A Pasture*).

ROOMS 10 and 11 gather two impressive painting collections—

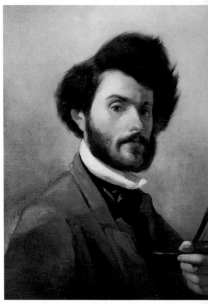

that of Cristiano Banti, donated by his heirs in 1958 (works include the *Women of the Woods* by Banti himself), and that of Diego Martelli, donated to the city in 1897 (works include *In Bed* by **F. Zandomeneghi** and *Landscape* by **C. Pissarro**).

The following ROOMS (12-17) display masterpieces that commemorate historical events, **S. Ussi** (*The Exile of the Duke of Athens*, 1862), and portraits from the time of Umberto I (**M. Gordigiani**, *Portrait of Gabriella Coujère, The Painter's Wife*).

ROOMS 18 to 20 gather works by Macchiaioli ("makers of patches") and post-Macchiaioli artists and by artists from other schools. These paintings were formerly held in Municipal deposits or were part of the Ambron Collection. Works by **G. Fattori** (*Stepdaughter's Portrait, Cousin Argia, The Southwesterly Gale*, and *The Palmieri Rotunda*) stand out. Paintings by **T. Signorini** (*September Morning in Settignano, Roofs in Riomaggiore, Leith*) and sculptures by **A. Cecioni** (*The Suicide*) also deserve special mention.

ROOMS 21 to 24 display naturalist paintings such as those by **A. Tommasi** (*Spring*) and **G. De Nittis** (*Rain of Ash*). There are also works by artists influenced by European culture (**O. Vermehren**, *Paolo and Francesca*, and **E. Gelli**, *Portrait of Bruna Pagliano*) as well as symbolist and divisionist paintings (the *Little Bacchus* by **P. Nomellini** and *In the Meadow* by **G. Previati**).

ROOMS 25 and 26 house collections of studies such as the *Emilio Gagliardini Collection* and include *The Tragic News* by **O. Borrani**, *Horses in the Pinewood of Tombolo* by Fattori, and *Noon* by Nomellini.

The last ROOMS (27-30) display decadent, symbolist, and post-impressionist works like *Intimacies* by **A. Spadini**, the *Portrait of Giovanni Papini* by **O. Ghiglia**, *Peace* by **G. Chini**, *The Good Smile* by **G. Costetti**.

MUSEO DEGLI ARGENTI (The Grand-Ducal Treasure)

This collection was placed on display in 1919 in the summer apartments of the Medici court so as to house the collection of precious objects and jewelry gathered over the centuries by the Medici and the Lorraines.

The 25 rooms, some of which are marvelously decorated by G. da San Giovanni (1635 ca.), are mainly grouped according to the type of objects they display (rock crystal, porcelain, amber, ivory, reliquaries, etc.). Make sure you visit the room dedicated to CAMEOS and JEWELRY. You'll find works like the *Cameo of Cosimo I* (1557-1562), the *Ovate with a Perspective of Piazza Signoria* (1599), and the *ex-voto of Cosimo II*; in the EXOTICISMS HALL and the LOGGETTA, you'll find objects from Africa

*Hall of G. da San
Giovanni*

*Flask designed by
Buontalenti*

*Augsburg Manufacture,
Cabinet known as
"d'Alemagna"*

"Master of the Furies,"
Curtius Riding his
Horse into the Abyss

V. Belli, Medici Chest

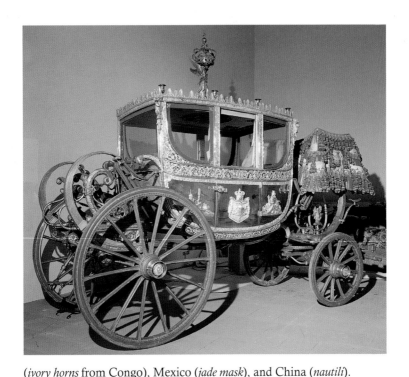

(*ivory horns* from Congo), Mexico (*jade mask*), and China (*nautili*).

The collections of Ferdinando III of Lorraine, called the *Treasure* of the prince-bishops of Salzburg and Würzburg (the portable altar, the series of 54 bowls in gilded silver, and the flask with grotesque art are all impressive), the *Treasure* of Anna Maria Luisa de' Medici (located in the jewelry room and includes some "bejeweled gallantries" with a curious collection of tiny animals from Flanders) as well as Lorenzo the Magnificent's *"Celadon" vases* (14th cent.) can be found here.

The last section of the museum, the HALL OF DONATIONS, gathers jewelry and objects (1600s-1900s) that were donated to the museum. Here you'll see the splendid *Diadem* by Cartier (1900) studded with amethysts and diamonds.

CARRIAGE MUSEUM (ground floor, temporarily closed to the public)

This museum displays the original carriage models that belonged to the Lorraine and the Savoy families (1700s-1800s), along with saddleries.
The early 19th-century carriage that belonged to Ferdinando II King of Naples stands out. It arrived with the Savoy family and is lavishly decorated in gilded silver.

COSTUME GALLERY

Set up in 1983 in the rooms of the PALAZZINA OF THE MERIDIAN (the Savoy family also resided here), this collection gathers over 6,000 items of clothing including centuries-old garments, theater costumes, and accessories (1700s-1900s). Many objects were donated or purchased. The funerary garments of Cosimo I de' Medici, Eleanor of Toledo, and their son Garzia are spectacular.

Silver carriage
Costume Gallery
Doccia Manufacture, Cup

PORCELAIN MUSEUM (Casino del Cavaliere, top part of Boboli Garden) Established in 1973, it collects porcelains that once belonged to the families that lived in Palazzo Pitti. Divided into 3 rooms, Italian and French porcelains are found in the first room (look for the Neapolitan biscuit figurines, and the Doccia and Sèvres tableware). Viennese porcelains are located in the second room, and pieces of Meissen manufacture can be found in the third.

Ice house, Boboli Garden
B. del Bianco (school of), Fruit
stands and baskets of fruit
with wine in an ice house,
Galleria Palatina (depository)

Ice gardens

Following the acquisition of the Palazzo Pitti, in 1549 Cosimo de' Medici commissioned Tribolo to design the Boboli Garden. The first year's work was very intensive and concentrated on organizing the park, the distribution of water and a full-scale fruit and vegetable activity, the produce of which was sold.

A number of architects succeeded each other in directing the work: Batista di Marco del Tasso, Bartolomeo Ammannati and, from 1569, Bernardo Buontalenti who created to the left of the palace the core of what would become the Giardino di Madama (wanted it seems by Giovanna d'Austria), with rare flowers and citrus trees.

Between the 16th and the 17th centuries the Boboli Garden became the prototype of the Italian garden, a veritably delightful place, where the princes liked to spend time surrounded by luxuriant vegetation, amid fragrant species, colorful flowers and exotic fruits. The play of water, automated fountains and picturesque corners contributed to making the setting more evocative, in particular the *Grotta Grande* which would be taken as a model all over Europe.

The so-called 'ice houses', which are believed to date from the 16th century deserve a special mention: they are small architectural structures covered by a cap (which can still be seen today) built in the coolest part of the Boboli Garden, intended for storing large blocks of ice coming from Abetone or from the Reno valley (both in the Apennine Mountains) and used for the preservation of meat, perishable foods and wine.

The use of ice was a real expression of luxury and power: used for making extravagant delicacies such as sorbets and ice creams, it also became the raw material for spectacular sculptures that became fascinating centerpieces at the Medici court's sumptuous banquets or spectacular scenic designs inside the grottoes of the Boboli Garden. Foremost among the artists who worked on these extravagant figures was Bernardo Buontalenti, who distinguished himself by his originality and skill: after preparing a model in wax he proceeded to sculpt the ice in great secrecy and in the cool of the Boboli ice house. Among his works are mentioned the reproductions of divinities and sea creatures accompanied by fishes and by the figure of Neptune. He is also credited with the invention of ice cream and innovative systems for the preservation during the summer months of ice, that he stored in his personal holes outside the walls.

Moreover, ice boasted highly therapeutic properties and its administration, which was guaranteed to the members of the court throughout all the seasons of the year in accordance with their position in the hierarchy, could actually be prescribed in the event of sickness by the court doctor, in the same way as rare and foreign wines and lemonades.

Nevertheless ice also had its detractors who discouraged its use because of its harmful effect of the undoubted 'frozen emotions'.

Boboli: *Fountain of the Artichoke and Amphitheater; Grand Grotto; Kaffeehaus; Mostaccini Fountain; Island Pond*

⑤

◇
5 BOBOLI GARDEN

This tour ends by crossing the BACCHUS COURTYARD into the Boboli Garden, which is a fine example of a Renaissance Italian garden. In 1549, Cosimo I asked **Tribolo** to design this green area, but it took many years to complete. Other architects who worked on the project include Ammannati, Buontalenti, and A. Parigi. It was finally completed in the late 1800s.

The expanse of the garden, 45,000 m. sq. between Palazzo Pitti, Forte Belvedere, and Porta Romana, had to reflect the Prince's power. In fact, this site became the preferred place for court games and performances. Today it offers visitors wonderful vistas of the city. If you stroll through the park, you'll see many statues, fountains, grottos, small ponds, and even an amphitheater.

At the garden's ENTRANCE you'll find the curious *Bacchus Fountain* (1560, also called "of the dwarf Morgante") by **V. Cioli** that portrays a dwarf (who resided at Cosimo I's court) on top of a turtle.

BUONTALENTI'S GROTTO (1583-1588) stands out for the originality of its niches; here you'll find the figures of *Paris and Helen*, by **Bandinelli**, with man-made stalactites and marine elements. In the past, Michelangelo's original *Prisoners* were found here (today you'll find the copies), while in the fresco by **Poccetti** you'll see a *Venus* by **Giambologna**.

Don't miss the AMPHITHEATER (17th cent.) right behind Ammannati's courtyard, with aedicules and steps. At the center, you'll find an *Egyptian obelisk* (1500 B.C.) from Luxor and a granite tub from the Baths of Caracalla.

Take the central path and you'll reach a pond with the *Fountain of the Pitchfork* at the center; on the left you'll reach the Kaffeehaus rococo pavilion (1776) that overlooks the city. (*PANORAMIC VIEW) From the KNIGHT'S GARDEN, with the *Fountain of Monkeys* at the center, head down towards the path that among cypress trees and statues will lead you to the HOLME SQUARE, a large pond created by G. and A. Parigi beginning in 1618. A sculptural group, portraying various subjects including *Perseus* and *Andromeda* by Giambologna, is immersed in

the water, whereas on the central holme, surrounded by a stone balustrade and small lemon trees, you'll find the *Ocean* fountain, a copy of an original by Giambologna. If you head back towards the main exit, you'll see the LAST ROTARY and the LEMON GROVE.

T. Titi (?), Little dog, *Palazzo Pitti (depository)*

Court dogs

Following a fashion that was widespread among the greatest courts of Europe, the Medici, from the 1500s, owned small and large pet dogs that were combed, festooned with ribbons and adorned with precious jewels by people, usually dwarfs, specially charged with their care. The pendants that were attached to the animals ears appear particularly curious, real ear-rings decorated with ribbons and lace.

Spaniels, pugs, Dalmatians and Bolognese dogs were often pictured alongside the ladies and the little princes of the Medici household, but occasionally they themselves were the subjects of the portraits.

Hunting dogs appear in pictures with everyday scenes or in works that deal specifically with the art of hunting, that today are preserved in the major Florentine museums and in particular the Palazzo Pitti. Molossian mastiffs, greyhounds, bloodhounds and griffons actually accompanied their noble owners in hunting and were always around during stays at the country houses.

Dog collars and leads, embellished by Medici coats of arms, silver plates, buckles and bells were even recorded in the register of the Medici Guardaroba alongside paintings, sculptures and objets d'art, as in the case of the inventory drawn up on the death of Grand Prince Ferdinando in 1713.

◇
6 "LA SPECOLA" ZOOLOGICAL MUSEUM (Via Romana, 17)

The Museum was founded in 1775 by Pietro Leopoldo. Here he established an astronomical and meteorological observatory called the "Specola". The Grand Duke aimed to gather in a single location the Medici's scientific collections (including books, treatises, and instruments). In addition to the zoological collections (recently enriched with the purchase of the Italian and African Arachnid collection), the circa 600 display cases contain *the collection of anatomical wax specimens* made by the ceroplastics school, which was located in the museum until 1895.

On the floor above you'll find the famous GALILEO TRIBUNE that Leopoldo I commissioned in 1841 on the occasion of the Conference of Italian Scientists. It is made up of a vestibule and a hemicycle-shaped room decorated with marble, mosaics, and frescoes by various artists.

◇
7 VIA MAGGIO

Among the 16th-century palazzos, look for no. 26. Here you'll find the *palazzo of Bianca Cappello* (lover and second wife of Francesco I de' Medici); it was refurbished for her by B. Buontalenti and presents on its façade graffitoed grotesque art and a traveler's hat, the family's coat-of-arms.

4- OLTRARNO and S. TRINITA

Palazzo Guadagni

◇
1 CHURCH OF S. FELICE IN PIAZZA

Mentioned in documents as early as 1066, the church as it appears today dates back to the 1300s. The unadorned façade, attributed to **Michelozzo**, and the sculpted portal stand out. Some of the works inside include: on the SIXTH altar to the right you'll find the painting *Madonna and Saints* (1520) by **R. del Ghirlandaio**; in the MAIN CHAPEL, a wooden *Crucifix* (Giotto school) and to the left, the fresco *St. Felix Helping St. Maximus*, begun by **G. da S. Giovanni** and completed by **Volterrano** in 1636.

PIAZZA S. SPIRITO

The square, surrounded by 15th-century palazzos, resembles a garden with a fountain at the center and it comes to life especially in the summer thanks also to the presence of many traditional restaurants nearby. Look for *Palazzo Guadagni*, a 16th-century construction that was perhaps designed by **Cronaca** for the Dei family; in fact, it served as a model for many palazzos that were built for the large arcaded loggia situated above.

The church's unadorned 18th-century façade faces the square. The church was begun in 1444 by **Brunelleschi,** but completed by his successors in 1487 when the dome was built. In the late 1400s, other famous artists like **G. da Sangallo** (sacristy) and **Cronaca** (vestibule) also worked here. The slender, two-story bell tower, topped by an elegant belfry, was finished in 1541 and designed by **B. d'Agnolo**, whereas B. Ammannati and A. Parigi completed the complex with the two cloisters between the 16th and 17th centuries.

The church INTERIOR is shaped like a Latin cross with 3 naves. The large dome is located at the center of the transept.

If you begin your visit from the RIGHT NAVE, you'll come across works from the 15th to 17th centuries. These include: CHAPEL IV, *Jesus Driving the Merchants out of the Temple* (1572) by **G. Stradano**; **G. Caccini**'s MAIN ALTAR with its marble enclosure and a dome-covered baldachin is Baroque in style and has semi-precious stones; heading towards the apse you'll see a wooden *Crucifix* attributed to **Michelangelo**. CHAPEL XII houses the lovely work by **Filippino Lippi** entitled *Madonna with Child and Young St. John, St. Martin, and St. Catherine Martyr* (1494). In CHAPEL XIV, you'll find the marble sarcophagus dedicated to Neri di Gino Capponi, attributed to Bernardo Rossellino (1458). In the APSE, CHAPEL XVII displays the polyptych by **M. di Banco**, *Madonna with Child and Four Saints* (1345 ca.),

whereas CHAPELS XIX and XX contain two signed and dated works by **A. Allori**, *The Martyr Saints* (1574) and *The Adulteress* (1577).

In the LEFT TRANSEPT you'll find, among the most important works, those in CHAPEL XXVI, such as the *Enthroned Madonna with Child and St. Thomas and St. Peter* by **C. Rosselli** (1482). The lovely CHAPEL XXVII, also called CORBINELLI CHAPEL, presents architecture and furnishings by **A. Sansovino** (1492). In CHAPEL XXX, there's the *Enthroned Madonna with Child and Saints* by **R. del Garbo**, embellished with a splendid period frame.

Proceed to the LEFT NAVE. CHAPEL XXXIV, with the *Madonna, St. Anne, and Other Saints* by **R.** and **M. del Ghirlandaio**, is of particular interest. Look above to see the magnificent 15th-century stained glass windows. You'll be able to access the VESTIBULE from a door located under the organ. This was built by **Cronaca** (1494) and is shaped like a rectangle with a coffered barrel vault depicting mythological figures and supported by 12 Corinthian columns.

The SACRISTY (access from the vestibule) is the work of G. da Sangallo and was built between 1489 and 1492. It contains paintings like the one on the altar facing the entrance, *St. Fiacre Heals the Sick* (1596) by **A. Allori**. In the FIRST CLOISTER (access from the vestibule), the frescoed lunettes portraying *Stories of Augustinians*, executed by various artists, stand out.

◇
3 CENACOLO DI S. SPIRITO (Piazza S. Spirito, 29) This 14th-century Augustinian refectory is noteworthy for its rectangular shape and for its exposed truss covering with Gothic mullioned windows. On one of the walls you'll find the splendid fresco with overlapping scenes of the *Crucifixion with Mary, The Pious Women, Longinus and Other Soldiers*, and the *Last Supper* (1365 ca.), attributed to **Orcagna**, though unfinished in a few sections. The FONDAZIONE ROMANO is also located here. This collection was donated to the city in 1946 by the antiques dealer Salvatore Romano; it includes statues, fragments of architecture, and other precious objects from pre-Romanesque times to the 15th century.

Church of S. Spirito:

A. Sansovino, Sacrament Altar

Michelangelo (attr.), Crucifixion

Filippino Lippi, Madonna with Child and Saints

Orcagna, Last Supper, Crucifixion, *Cenacolo di S. Spirito*

Church of S. Maria del Carmine, *Brancacci Chapel:*

Masaccio, Expulsion from the Garden of Eden; The Tribute Money

Masaccio and Filippino Lippi, Resurrection of the Son of Theophilus and St. Peter on His Throne

Masolino, The Healing of the Cripple and the Resurrection of Tabitha

Corsini Chapel

90

4 CHURCH OF S. MARIA DEL CARMINE

The church, founded by the Carmelites in 1268, still bears the ruins of a Romanesque-Gothic structure. The church was refurbished over the centuries, and was finally completed in 1775 by G. Mannaioni.

The INTERIOR, with its frescoed ceilings, is in the shape of a Latin cross with 1 nave and 5 chapels on each side with decorated altars. Special mention must be made of CHAPEL III with its *Crucifixion* (1560) by **Vasari**.

In the MAIN CHAPEL, with its *ciborium* in marble and semi-precious stones, you'll find the *funerary Monument of Piero Soderini*, a sculpture by **B. da Rovezzano** (1513). From the LEFT TRANSEPT you'll reach the *Corsini Chapel*, a square-shaped, Roman Baroque-style room completed in 1683 by P.F. Silvani for Marquis Bartolomeo and Neri. Three funerary monuments are located inside, as well as many works by **G.B. Foggini**, including the *urn* with the body of S. Andrea Corsini.

BRANCACCI CHAPEL (access from the door to the right of the church) - The chapel is especially renowned for its frescoes by **Masaccio** and **Masolino**.

Felice Brancacci commissioned these works to Masolino and Masaccio in around 1423. Both artists worked together on this project up until 1428 (ca.). With the banishment of Felice Brancacci (1436) and Masaccio's untimely death, the work continued slowly. It was then decided that the chapel would be dedicated to the *Madonna of the People*. In fact, the 13th-century panel portraying the *Madonna*, which can sill be found on the altar, was brought here. This work is attributed to **C. di Marcovaldo**.

Lippi, Resurrection of the Son of Theophilus and St. Peter on His Throne *(detail)*

Filippino Lippi completed the frescoes in 1480; the themes of the *Original Sin* and *Episodes from the Life of St. Peter* follow one another. Certain scenes deserve special mention: *Temptation of Adam and Eve* by **Masolino**; the highly dramatic *Expulsion from the Garden of Eden* by **Masaccio** is considered the starting point of Renaissance painting. Next you'll see the most celebrated episode of the entire cycle: *Tribute Money* by Masaccio. Then: *St. Peter Preaching* by Masolino; the *Baptism of the Neophytes* by Masaccio; the *Resurrection of the Son of Theophilus and St. Peter on His Throne* by Masaccio and

Filippino Lippi. This is considered the last episode Masaccio painted before he moved to Rome; the portraits of many of his contemporaries are rather interesting. Look for Brunelleschi, Alberti, Masaccio, and Masolino. The final scenes are by Filippino: *The Dispute with Simon Mago, The Crucifixion of St. Peter* (you can see the painter's self-portrait in the first episode—he is the young man with a hat on the far right; instead, in the second episode you'll find the *portrait of Sandro Botticelli*, Filippino's teacher—he is the person at the center of the group on the right who looks at the observer), and finally the *Angel Freeing St. Peter from Prison*.

◇
5 Church of S. Frediano in Cestello

This church, with its unfinished façade, was built between 1680 and 1689 by the Roman architect Cerutti. It is adorned with a dome by A. Ferri (1698) and a bell tower. The INTERIOR, in the form of a Latin cross with 1 nave, stands out for its Baroque style and small side chapels. A must-see: the dome's decorations by D. Gabbiani and the impressive 18th-century MAIN ALTAR in marble and semi-precious stones. In the LEFT TRANSEPT, you'll find the *Crucifixion and Saints* by **J. del Sellaio**.

◇
6 Palazzo Corsini and Gallery (Lungarno Corsini, 10) (*panoramic view)

Designed by P.F. Silvani (1656), this palazzo is home to the CORSINI GALLERY collection (visits must be scheduled in advance), begun in 1765 by Father Lorenzo Corsini. It contains masterpieces by artists from Florence, Italy, and abroad (1400s-1700s).

Ponte alla Carraia

◇ 7 PALAZZO SPINI-FERONI

Erected in the late 1200s to defend the bridge S. Trinita, you'll be amazed by this massive, three-story, embattled construction. It was refurbished various times and, until 1824, it also had a tower and an arch. Since 1995 the SALVATORE FERRAGAMO MUSEUM has been located here; this museum contains 10,000 shoe models created by the maison from the 1920s to today. Historical documents like films and photos round off the collection.

◇ 8 BASILICA OF S. TRINITA

This church is located in Piazza S. Trinita. At the center of the square you'll find the *Column of Justice*. The basilica was built by Vallombrosian monks in the second-half of the 11th century. It was later enlarged and modified in Gothic style during the early 1300s. Work was finally concluded in the early 15th century. The Baroque stone façade was designed by B. Buontalenti. The INTERIOR has a Gothic layout in the form of an Egyptian cross with 3 naves. In the RIGHT NAVE, CHAPEL IV stands out: it is

closed off by an iron gate and contains frescoes by **L. Monaco** (1425) depicting *episodes from the Virgin's life*. This same artist also executed the panel with the *Annunciation* located on the ALTAR.

In the RIGHT TRANSEPT, in the *Sassetti Chapel* you can admire the cycle of frescoes by **D. Ghirlandaio** with *Stories of St. Francis of Assisi* (1486). Important figures of the age (Francesco Sassetti and his son, Lorenzo de' Medici, Agnolo Poliziano with the Magnificent's children) and sights such as Piazza S. Trinita, Palazzo Spini, and Palazzo della Signoria can be seen. Take note of Ghirlandaio's *Adoration of the Shepherds* on the altar.

D. Ghirlandaio, Sassetti Chapel
L. della Robbia, Tomb of Benozzo Federighi

In the PRESBYTERY, few fragments of a cycle painted by A. Baldovinetti of stories taken from the Old Testament can be seen. In the LEFT TRANSEPT, in CHAPEL II, look for the *Tomb of Benozzo Federighi, Bishop of Fiesole* (1454) in marble with multi-colored majolica tiles by **L. della Robbia**. The CHAPEL WITH THE RELICS OF ST. GIOVANNI GUALBERTO, decorated by **Passignano** with scenes related to the veneration of this saint's relics, is right nearby.

In the LEFT NAVE, in CHAPEL V, the wooden statue depicting *Magdalene* by **D. da Settignano** is rather impressive. Make sure you stop by CHAPEL IV to see the tomb of the medieval Florentine chronicler Dino Compagni.

◇ 9 VIA DE' TORNABUONI

This is Florence's most elegant and famous street with fashionable shops and lovely Renaissance palazzos. Look for: *Palazzo Minerbetti* (Via de' Tornabuoni, no. 3), *Palazzo Strozzi del Poeta* (no. 5), an example of Baroque architecture by **G. Silvani**, *Circolo dell'Unione* (no. 7) by **Vasari** but based on a project by **Giambologna**, *Palazzo Corsi* (no. 16), a 15th-century building by **Michelozzo** with a loggia refurbished by **Cigoli** in 1608.

◇◇ 10 CHURCH OF S. GAETANO (Piazza Antinori)

Dedicated to the order of the Theatins, this church is an exquisite example of Baroque art (1638). The interior is covered in black marble.

11 CHURCH OF S. MARIA MAGGIORE (Piazza di S. Maria Maggiore)

Among the oldest of the city's churches, it was founded before the 11th century and rebuilt in the Gothic style in the second half of the 1200s for the Vallombrosani. On the simple façade that gives onto the piazza, you can see the coat of arms of the Panciatichi family.

The INTERIOR, with three naves with pointed arches, ends with three chapels. It was restructured several times over the centuries by various architects (among them G. Silvani and Cigoli) and today is the product of the latest restoration of 1912. Note the late 14th-century frescoes attributed to **M. di Nardo**, *S. Alberto saving two Jews* (1596) by **Cigoli**, and in the SECOND CHAPEL, the work *S. Rita da Cascia* (1949) by **P. Conti**. Brunetto Latini, Dante's master, is buried here.

☺ LA BERTA (Church of S. Maria Maggiore - Via Cerretani)

> *On the bell tower of this old church you can see a marble bust. A popular tale says that the head depicts a fruit-seller called Berta who had her stall nearby. She decided to leave all her belongings to the monks for them to set up a bell that would alert the farmworkers in the fields before the city gates were closed. Others though, say that it's the petrified head of a monk. He's supposed to have appeared at a small window when an astrologer, deemed to be a heretic and condemned to death, was passing by, and to have shouted not to give him anything to drink, as he was requesting, because he should have been able to save his life by means of his magical powers. The condemned man then responded that he would never leave that spot and the monk's head petrified instantly.*

12 PIAZZA AND PALAZZO STROZZI

The palazzo of the merchant Filippo Strozzi the Elder was built here in the late 1400s. **B. da Maiano**'s project consisted in a cube-shaped structure with ashlar work and 3 identical sides. It was Cronaca who carried on the project between 1502 and 1503, adding the protruding cornice and the courtyard with a collumned arcade and loggia.

Giambologna, 'Diavolino'

Refurbishment, however, was definitively suspended in 1538. In fact, the south façade and half of the cornice were never completed. Take note of the wrought iron finishings like the flag and horse poles, iron lamps, and bands for torches and banners around the construction

Today, this palazzo is State property. A few of the halls have been set aside for exhibitions. Also located here is the *Gabinetto G. P. Vieusseux*. Founded by the Swiss merchant Giovan Pietro Vieusseux in 1819, it possesses a vast library (about 650,000 volumes) open to the public as well as a restoration workshop.

☺ **Il Diavolino** (Via Strozzi – corner of Via de'Vecchietti)

A miraculous event that took place in 1245 is associated with this standard holder, a work in bronze by Giambologna. It's said that during a sermon by S. Pietro Martire against heretics, the Devil suddenly appeared right there in the Piazza della Repubblica in the form of a black runaway horse. To prevent harm from coming to the faithful, the monk made the sign of the cross towards the animal and it stopped, vanishing at the exact point where you see the 'Diavolino' today.

13 Piazza della Repubblica

This square was built between 1885 and 1895 on top of the centuries-old constructions of the Mercato Vecchio and in the area that once was the Roman forum. Overall, the square today seems like an elegant open-air lounge area with its very refined cafés. However, this square was originally home to the Jewish ghetto, Vasari's Loggia del Pesce (to-

day located in Piazza dei Ciompi), and various private residences.
V. Micheli is also credited with the triumphal arch and its series of porticos.
In 1951, the *Column of Abundance* was erected here; this column marks the spot where the Roman *decumanus* and *cardus* once met.

◇◇
14 LOGGIA OF THE MERCATO NUOVO (New Market)

Also called the Loggia *of straw* or *del Porcellino* for the fountain that portrays a boar (a bronze copy of the original by **P. Tacca)**.
The loggia, square in shape, was commissioned by Cosimo I to G. B. del Tasso (1551). Goods from the most important guilds of the age would be sold here. During the 19th century, statues were added to beautify the loggia. Today, you'll find many stands that sell handmade Florentine products.
In the evening, when the area is empty, look for a marble wheel at the center, that indicates where the 'Carroccio' was positioned before battles in the Middle Ages, and where merchants charged with fraudulent bankruptcy were put on show before the public.

☺ IL PORCELLINO (✋)

> *There's a tradition that if you want to come back to Florence you have to 'feed' the Piglet with a coin; it has to be placed on the animal's tongue and allowed to slide down. If the coin falls into the grating below, you'll be back soon.*

15 PIAZZA DI PARTE GUELFA

A small medieval section of the center, the former church of Santa Maria Sopraporta (today a library) and the PALAGIO DEI CAPITANI DI PARTE GUELFA, which was formerly the headquarters of the magistracy of Guelph captains, are located here. The 14th-century building was enlarged by Brunelleschi and Vasari and refurbished in the early 1900s. Today, the Calcio Storico Fiorentino has its offices here. It also hosts various temporary exhibitions and cultural events.

16 CHURCH OF SS. APOSTOLI (Piazza del Limbo)

The church, built on what was the cemetery for babies who had died without being baptized and from which the piazza derives its name, has its origins in the distant past, possibly being founded in 800 by Charlemagne as a Medieval inscription on the Romanesque façade indicates; but it was certainly in existence in 1075. The INTERIOR has three naves with marble columns, the first two capitals of which come from the nearby Roman baths, and the ceiling is trussed in painted wood. Among the works of art, notice the polychrome glazed terracotta *tabernacle* by **G. della Robbia** and the funeral monuments, among them the *Sepulchre of Oddo Altoviti* (1510 ca.), by **B. da Rovezzano**, who also sculpted the *holy water stoup* to the left and the portal. In the RECTORY there is a fire holder in gilded copper and silver where flint fragments of the Holy Sepulcher are kept, brought back by Pazzino de'Pazzi on his return from the first Crusade (1099) to the Holy Land. Even today at Easter they are still taken in procession to the DUOMO and used to light the fire for the 'Scoppio del Carro', or explosion of the cart.

17 PALAZZO DAVANZATI (Piazza Davanzati)

Museum of the Ancient Florentine House - It was built by the Davizzi family (merchants) in the 1300s, but passed on to the Davanzati family in 1578, who lived here until 1838. After various owners, this palazzo became State property and in 1956 a museum was opened here. What might catch your eye are the iron objects on the façade that were once used to tie horses, "erri," or rather, rods used to hang laundry or bird traps, and torch or flag holders on the

Lo Scheggia, Il gioco del civettino, *Museum of the Ancient Florentine House*

sides of the windows. This museum displays
furnishings (chests, beds, credenzas, tables, refectory chairs), paintings, statues, tapestries, and
everyday objects (basins, pitchers, plates, lamps,
looms, irons) of a typical 14th-century family.
The lively decorations on the walls will certainly
delight you. Make sure you see the PARROT and
PEACOCK ROOMS.

◇◇
18 PIAZZA DE' RUCELLAI

Shaped like a triangle, this square was designed by
L.B. Alberti during the second-half of the 1400s.
Palazzo Rucellai, built in various phases between
1455 and 1470 by B. Rossellino and designed by Alberti himself, looks out onto the square. The Alinari
photo archives and the FRATELLI ALINARI MUSEUM OF
PHOTOGRAPHY HISTORY (now in Piazza Santa Maria
Novella, 14a) were once located here. This museum
gathers antique cameras and photo equipment and
hosts temporary photo exhibitions. In front of the
palazzo you'll see the LOGGIA DE' RUCELLAI with 3
arches with the family's coats-of-arms (rings with
diamonds and feathers and sails); in the past, family
celebrations were held in this loggia.

Wine and taverns in Florence

In the Florence of Dante and Boccaccio the consumption of wine was so widespread that its sale was a major source of profit for the agricultural economy and for the Municipality that levied a duty on it: you need only consider that the average amount consumed each day, for each of the city's 100,000 inhabitants, was more than a liter.

Moreover, in the Middle Ages (and again in the following centuries) a vast range of therapeutic properties was ascribed to wine, which, viewed as a source of nutrition, as an excellent digestive and tonic, as an adjuvant in the production of blood and as an antidote against melancholy, was prescribed for women, particularly when about to give birth, for the elderly and for children; its administration and the alcohol content increased depending on the age, the mood or the nature of the person. Moreover, because of its hygienic qualities its use was recommended in hospitals and, in moderate amounts, in convents and monasteries too. However it was forbidden for the clergy to visit the taverns and inns, places that anyway by law had to be located at a distance from holy places and had to adjust their opening hours to take account of the times of the liturgy.

Wine was also consumed in abundance during work; the employers on building sites, for example, offered it to the workers and on large sites, such as for example during construction of the dome of the Duomo directed by Brunelleschi, in the morning large baskets containing food for lunch and many demijohns of wine were hoisted up (and maybe this was why every now and then a worker fell off the scaffolding).

The most common wine was the 'vermiglio', or red, although the most sought after was the white and in particular the 'trebbiano'; imported liqueur-like wines were highly regarded, such as 'vino greco' or Greek wine, 'vernaccia', 'malvasia', and 'vino cotto'.

The wines sold in Florence arrived mainly from the countryside: from upper Valdarno came the best 'trebbiano' and the 'vermiglio', while 'Chianti' came from all of the surrounding area, including Valdigreve, Bagno a Ripoli and Rignano sull'Arno.

Wine distribution in Florence was widespread: the principal vendors were the wine merchants, followed by bakers, inn-keepers, tavern-keepers and hoteliers, but the farmers and producers could also engage in the retail trade. It's important to remember that the major wine producers were often bankers and merchants belonging to the most prominent Florentine families, who selected farm properties as a means of investment and who carried out wine retailing from the noble dwellings of the city through the characteristic wickets and little windows; even the Medici, during the course of the 1400s, gave over part of their estates of Cafaggiolo and Trebbio to viticulture.

Cellars, hostelries and taverns were scattered throughout medieval Florence, even though the greatest concentration was to be found among the people of S. Maria Maggiore, near the Mercato Vecchio (today the Piazza della Repubblica), where among the vendors' stalls you would come across the assorted customers of the hostelries seated at the tables.

The wine merchants were prohibited from selling food that would make people thirsty, such as herb fritters, even though some little snack was probably served nevertheless; in the taverns and the hostelries food was more freely available, although the prohibition on offering tidbits and savory dishes applied there also. Nevertheless there are numerous accounts from those days that describe the Florentines' custom of regularly eating at the hostelries.

Games of chance, such as cards or dice, were often played in the taverns, but then were outlawed during the Medici era, along with prostitution, which was fairly common in this type of establishment. The hostelries were the main meeting places both for Florentines and for foreigners, and were often frequented by artists too, among them being Michelangelo himself. But there were also those who gave up the 'sophistries and distillations of the brain' of art in order to open a hostelry, such as Mariotto Albertinelli, the painter from the 1500s who is still commemorated today in Via Dante Alighieri by a plaque at the *Pennello* trattoria.

Some taverns spanned the entire history of Florence from the Middle Ages to the 19th century, becoming famous for the delicacies that could be enjoyed there; among the oldest we could mention the *Taverna delle Bertucce,* the following Osterias *del Porco, del Fico, della Malvagia, di Vinegia, dei Pentolini, della Gatta, Coroncina* and *al Frascato*.

Even today strolling through Florence it is possible to spot the little windows or wickets in some of the genteel residences that were used in olden days for selling wine. Situated by the cellar, they were just the right size to allow a flask to be passed through. The 'buchette del vino' or little wine holes, framed in stone with a little shutter to close them, were also used by the owners of the buildings for making gifts of charity, at times food and wine for the most poor being found inside them. The Florentine streets where the largest number of 'buchette' can be found are Borgo degli Albizi, Borgo Pinti, Piazza S. Croce, Via degli Alfani, Via Bardi, and Via S. Spirito.

A. Allori, Cleopatra's Banquet, *Palazzo Vecchio*

5. S. MARIA NOVELLA and OGNISSANTI

[Map of the S. Maria Novella and Ognissanti area of Florence, with labeled streets and locations including STAZIONE S. MARIA NOVELLA, PIAZZA DELLA STAZIONE, S. M. NOVELLA, PIAZZA SANTA MARIA NOVELLA, PIAZZA D'OGNISSANTI, S. LORENZO, PIAZZA DELLA REPUBBLICA, and numbered points 1–5]

◇
1 S. MARIA NOVELLA TRAIN STATION

The train station is located behind the Basilica of S. Maria Novella. It was built between 1933 and 1935 and is based upon a project by the "Gruppo Toscano," directed by G. Michelucci. It was intended to be a modern structure in *pietra forte* in perfect harmony with the centuries-old constructions surrounding it. The inside roof is made of glass; the floor is in marble and serpentine and there are many benches, baggage rests, and small bronze drinking fountains. You'll find 2 tempera landscape paintings by **O. Rosai** on the walls.

PIAZZA S. MARIA NOVELLA

This is one of the loveliest squares in Florence. It was begun in 1287 by will of the commune and completed around 40 years later. It acted as the center of religious activities and public life (the *palio dei Cocchi*, a horserace that involved riding around the 2 marble obelisks supported by 4 turtles made by Giambologna, was held here starting in 1563).

Facing the square are the Church of S. Maria

G. Signorini, Palio dei cocchi in Piazza Santa Maria Novella, *Gallery of Modern Art, Pitti Palace*

Novella and the LOGGIA OF THE HOSPITAL OF S. PAOLO, a 13th-century foundation offering medical assistance; it was suppressed by Grand Duke Pietro Leopoldo in 1780. Between the arches of the building you'll find glazed terracotta medallions depicting saints by **A. della Robbia**.

2 BASILICA OF S. MARIA NOVELLA

The origins of this complex date back to 1221 when a few Dominican friars took up residence in the church of S. Maria delle Vigne (11th cent.). A new church was then built in 1278. The work, carried out by the friar architects Sisto and Ristoro, were completed in the mid-14th century. Even though the Gothic façade remained incomplete, the church was consecrated by Pope Martin V in 1420. On the occasion of the 1439 Council, plans were made to finish the façade, and with funds from the wealthy Florentine, Giovanni Rucellai, Alberti was entrusted with the task. He integrated the already-present Gothic elements into his typically Renaissance design. The result is exceptional. In fact, there is a continuity of color and proportion. Observe the beautiful triangular tympanum with a sun, the symbol of the Dominicans. Among the details Alberti added there are the frieze with the name of Giovanni Rucellai and the date, 1470, as well as the family's coat-of-arms. In 1574, a gnomon on the right and an armillary sphere on the left were added.

The INTERIOR, transformed various times, is in the shape of a Latin cross with 3 naves divided by columns in *pietra forte*. It's one of Florence's most prestigious sights for the quantity and quality of its art (works by Giotto,

Orcagna, Brunelleschi, Masaccio, and Filippino Lippi). You'll find an endless succession of chapels. Some of the most important ones include: RIGHT NAVE: (bay II) *Tomb of the Blessed Villana* (1451) by **B. Rossellino** and **D. da Settignano**; (bay VI) CHAPEL OF THE PURE, built by the Ricasoli family in 1473 to house the miraculous image of the Madonna, venerated by Florentine mothers. At the end of the nave on the right, go up the steps and you'll reach the RUCELLAI CHAPEL: on the altar you'll find the *Madonna with Child*, a marble sculpture by **N. Pisano** (mid-14th cent.). In the transept on the right, you'll see the BARDI CHAPEL with its iron gate and lamps from the 1700s; there's also a painting on the right pillar of *St. Gregory Blessing the Founder of the Chapel*, while on the altar you'll see the *Madonna of the Rosary* (1570) by **Vasari**. In the FILIPPO STROZZI CHAPEL, decorated with frescoes (1502) by **Filippino Lippi**, observe the *Tomb of Filippo Strozzi* by **B. da Maiano**. In the MAIN CHAPEL or the TORNABUONI CHAPEL, dedicated to Our Lady of the Assumption, you'll see the *cycle of frescoes* (1490) by **D. del Ghirlandaio** and in the sacred scenes (including the *Life of the Virgin*, *Stories of St. John the Baptist*, the *Evangelists*), you'll recognize many famous figures of the age. Under the paintings there's the inlaid wooden *chorus* by **B. d'Agnolo**. On the altar you'll find a bronze *Crucifix* by **Giambologna**. The GONDI CHAPEL, covered with marble and porphyry by **G. da Sangallo** (1503), is famous for the *Crucifix* by **Brunelleschi**, this artist's only work in wood. Then there's the GADDI CHAPEL, in marble and semi-precious stones and decorated with frescoes depicting the *Episodes from*

Filippino Lippi, Filippo Strozzi Chapel

the *Life of St. Jerome* and the *Virtues* by **A. Allori**. In the LEFT TRANSEPT, you'll find the STROZZI CHAPEL (of Mantua) with *frescoes* (1350-1377) by **N. di Cione** inspired by Dante's *Divine Comedy*, which is represented on the left; on the altar, there's the panel *Christ Risen Giving the Keys to St. Peter and a Book to St. Thomas, the Madonna, St. John the Baptist, and Other Saints* (1357) by **Orcagna**. In the Gothic SACRISTY, observe the lavabo in marble and glazed terra-cotta by **G. della Robbia**, relic cabinets designed by Buontalenti, and a wooden *Crucifix* by **Giotto** at the entrance. In the LEFT NAVE (bay IV), look for the *Trinity* fresco with the *Madonna, St. John, and the Patrons Lenzi Kneeling Down* by **Masaccio** (1427 ca.), a fundamental work in which the artist applied the teachings of Brunelleschi's mathematical perspective. Nearby you'll also see a lovely marble *pulpit* (1462) by Brunelleschi.

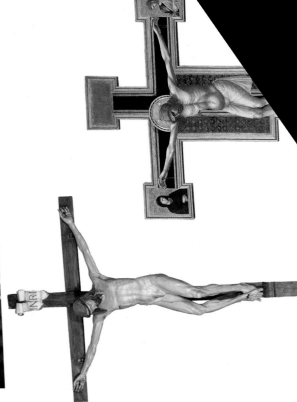

D. Ghirlandaio, The Naming of John the
Baptist, Tornabuoni Chapel

Masaccio, Trinity

N. di Cione, Strozzi di Mantova Chapel

F. Brunelleschi, Crucifixion

Giotto, Crucifixion

Green Cloister
P. Uccello, Episodes from the Genesis and
the Life of Noah
A. di Bonaiuto, Triumph of St. Thomas
Aquinas, Spanish Chapel

S. Maria Novella Museum of Sacred Art and the Cloisters

This museum is chiefly composed of the cloisters and the refectory annexed to the basilica.

Green Cloister: Built by **Fra' J. Talenti** (1332-1350 and after) and surrounded by lowered round arches, it was frescoed by **P. Uccello** with *Creation Stories* (1425-1430) using mostly green paint. Observe the *Creation of the Animals*, the *Original Sin*, *Noah's Ark*, the *Universal Flood*, and the *Drunkenness of Noah*. Capitular Hall or Spanish Chapel - In 1540, Eleanor of Toledo created this chapel for the many noble Spaniards in her court; it's rectangular in shape with a single cross vault held up by large arches. The vault and the walls are frescoed by **A. di Buonaiuto** with a cycle depicting the zealous activity of the Dominicans in combating heresies. Some episodes include *St. Peter Sailing*, the *Resurrection*, the *Pentecost*, the *Militant and Triumphant Church*, and the *Triumph of St. Thomas Aquinas*.

Cloister of the Dead - This area was already present when the friars arrived. It is a colonnade on 2 sides with octagonal pillars and cross... Here you'll find the *funerary chapel of the Strozzi family* with fres...cagna's pupils.

Refectory - It hosts the Museum of Sacred Art where ...include... belonged to the Dominican friars. The ... by **P. ...**cred wall hangings. Look for the ... case ... of St. Orsola, the rock crystal ... by A... Cross, and the *Last Supper* ... by ... Main Cloister and ...

Officina Profumo-Farmaceutica di Santa Maria Novella

Anyone traveling to Florence today must not fail to visit the 'Officina Profumo-Farmaceutica di Santa Maria Novella', or Perfume-Pharmaceutical Workshop of Santa Maria Novella, located in Via della Scala. A modern-day Palace of delights, and an oasis of silence and perfumes, the Officina has been able to keep intact that insistence on quality of the raw materials, of the work and of the environment over the centuries have made the boundary between Florentine work such a fine line created from a part of the old convent, pharmacy, charge by prior appointment. Tradesman modified the chapel of S. Niccolò in Basle from the fa from the 1300s, was in the neo-Gothic style starting in 1848 in order to provide a suitable welcome to the famous personages who visited it.

The old grocer's shop, used from the 17th to the 19th centuries for the sale of the products, has largely retained its original appearance and in the cupboards it is still possible to see the old apothecary equipment with jars, mortars, scientific instruments, old recipe books and a book for the signatures of its illustrious visitors.

The Sacristy of S. Niccolò ends the visit, its walls frescoed with scenes drawn from the *Passion of Christ*; the pictures, attributed to Mariotto di Nardo were carried out probably between 1385 and 1405. In the 1600s the Chapel was used as a room for storing 'distilled' water and hence came to be known as the water room.

The activity of the Officina Profumo-Farmaceutica di Santa Maria Novella, closely linked to that of the neighboring Dominican Monastery of the same name, has its origin in the religious ideal of charity practiced through the care and assistance of the sick.

From 1221 onwards the monks, using the medicinal plants grown in the gardens of their monastery, laid the foundations for the apothecary's activity, often taking advantage of the collaboration of expert secular chemists, while the art of fragrances developed from 1381.

From the 17th century the preparation of perfume-medicinal specialties was radically revived by new elements and skills, the fruit of recent scientific research and technological progress; for this reason 1612 has been identified as the year when the Officina was officially founded. During the course of the 1600s the fame of the Farmacia spread abroad beyond the borders of the grand duchy, due more than anything else to the perfumed waters, the creams, the soaps and the fragrant scents that the sophisticated foreign traveler coming to Florence made certain of buying.

In the 18th century the Officina's renown grew still further, so much so that numerous requests for remedies arrived even from China; moreover, these years saw the invention of the booze alkermes, which remained its biggest selling specialty until the end of the 1800s.

Following the suppression of the religious orders carried out by the Italian state in 1866, the Officina became a completely lay and private business.

The Officina established excellent relations with the Medici family, which granted it privileges, honors and the title of the 'Fonderia di sua Altezza Reale' or Distillery of His Royal Highness, as well as numerous gifts, among them a panel by Matteo Rosselli depicting the Dominican Saint Pietro from Verona, patron saint of the Farmacia.

the School of Petty Officers and can be visited only upon authorization. The chapel hosted Pope Leo x de' Medici in 1515 and was frescoed on that occasion by **R. Ghirlandaio** and **Pontormo**, who painted the *Veronica* here.

◇
3 Borgo Ognissanti

Walking along this street, try to find no. 26. Here you'll see the *Casa-galleria* (House-Gallery), created in 1911 by the architect **G. Michelazzi,** a rare example of art nouveau architecture in Florence.

◇
4 Church of Ognissanti

The most important construction in Piazza Ognissanti is the church founded in 1251 by the order of the Humiliati, dedicated wool weavers. Due to its proximity to the Arno and many mills and workshops, this was an ideal site for the friars' activity.

The bell tower is medieval, whereas the façade, refurbished in 1637 by M. Nigetti, is Baroque. Observe the city's emblem and the lunette above the portal with the *Crowning of Mary and Saints* in glazed terracotta.

The INTERIOR consists in a single nave with a transept. On ALTAR II to the right, you'll find frescoes by **D. Ghirlandaio** depicting the *Pietà*, *Deposition from the Cross*, and the *Madonna of Mercy*. On ALTAR III there's the panel of the *Madonna and Saints* by **Santi di Tito** (1565), and then the lovely fresco by **Botticelli**, *St. Augustine in His Study* (1480 ca.). Almost in front of this work you'll see *St. Jerome in His Study* by Ghirlandaio. In the CHAPEL after altar I in the right transept, you'll find on the floor the marble tomb of Botticelli and his family, the Filipepi. The MAIN ALTAR (1593-1595) was made by **J. Ligozzi** in semi-precious stones; the bronze *Crucifix* is by **G. B. Cennini** (17th cent.).

In the SACRISTY, observe the fragments of 14th-century frescoes by **T. Gaddi** and the painted *Cross* (Giotto's pupils). The religious complex ends with a cloister and refectory where you can admire a *Last Supper* by **Ghirlandaio**.

D. Ghirlandaio, Madonna of Mercy; Mourning Over the Dead Christ; St Jerome in His Study
Botticelli, St. Agustine in His Study
D. Ghirlandaio, Last Supper

◇
5 MARINO MARINI MUSEUM (Piazza di S. Pancrazio)
Inaugurated in 1988 in the former Church of S. Pancrazio, it gathers the collection of the artist **Marini** (1901-1980). The former church was divided into 3 floors, and the works were arranged according to year and theme. Paintings include *The Virgins* (1920), an oil on canvas clearly influenced by Piero della Francesca and Masaccio, the *Lansquenet*, the *Jugglers* (1954). Don't miss the following works: *Victory* (1928, plaster cast), the *Swimmer* (in wood), the *Horse* (in bronze), and *Anita* (1943, in terracotta).

115

6. S. LORENZO and the MEDICI CHAPELS

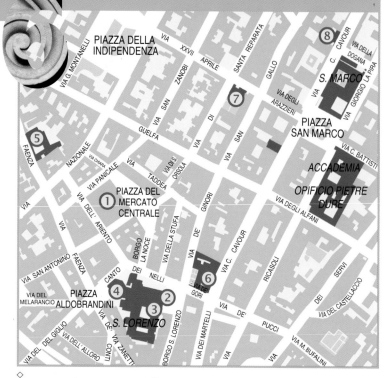

1 MARKET OF S. LORENZO (✋)

One of the most important glass and iron structures built by G. Mengoni in 1874, it was intended as a place where food could be bought and sold. It exists even today.

PIAZZA S. LORENZO

This vast square, famous for its market, is set off by the Church of S. Lorenzo and by lovely palaces (15th-16th cent.) including the celebrated *Palazzo Lotteringhi della Stufa* (no. 4). In front of the church you'll see the *Monument to Giovanni of the Black Bands* (1540), a Medici family forefather, by **B. Bandinelli**.

2 BASILICA OF S. LORENZO

Consecrated in 393 by St. Ambrose, it is dedicated to the martyr Lawrence. It was the city's first cathedral until the 8th century. The basilica was rebuilt in Romanesque style and re-consecrated in 1059. In 1418, the Medici family became its official patrons and decided to completely refurbish it at their own expense and with contributions from other powerful families in the area, who would then be given a chapel inside the basilica. The work was commissioned to Brunelleschi, who presented his designs in 1421 to Giovanni de' Medici, the city's Gonfalonier. The church was completed in 1461. A library and the mausoleum of the Chapel of Princes were then added. The INTERIOR, despite the 19th-century refurbishment, is harmonious with its decorations in *pietra serena*. This basilica houses

rather important works. Starting in the RIGHT NAVE observe CHAPEL II: *Marriage of the Virgin* (1523) by **R. Fiorentino,** and between the last chapel in the right nave and the transept you'll find the marble *Altar of the Sacrament* (1460 ca.) by **D. da Settignano**. Under the 2 final arches of the central nave you'll admire 2 bronze *pulpits* by **Donatello**; these are in the shape of an ark that rests upon Ionic columns. In the MAIN CHAPEL: the semi-precious stone altar made by the Opificio delle pietre dure (1787). LEFT TRANSEPT, CHAPEL I: wooden sculpture by **G. Fetti** portraying the *Madonna with Child*. In CHAPEL II, observe the altarpiece, the *Abbot St. Anthony on a Throne with St. Lawrence and St. Giuliano,* from the workshop of **D. Ghirlandaio**.
OLD SACRISTY - You'll reach the Old Sacristy from the back of the left transept. It was built by Brunelleschi (1421-1426) as a chapel for Giovanni de' Medici. Decorations were entrusted to Donatello who created the *bas-reliefs* with angels, the large lunettes above the entrances, the lavabos depicting (on the right) *St. Cosmas and St. Damian* (patron saints of the Medici family) and *St. Lawrence and St. Stephen* (on the left), the *tondos* on the walls with the *Evangelists,* and the *pendentives* with *Stories of St. John the Evangelist*. At the center of the room you'll see the *tomb of Giovanni di Bicci de' Medici and his wife Piccarda Bueri* by **A. il Baggiano**, with festoons, angels, and the Medici coat-of-arms. To the left there's the funerary monument to Piero and Giovanni de' Medici, Cosimo the Elder's son, dating to 1472; it is chiseled in porphyry by Verrocchio. On the apse vault, the position of the painted stars indicates the date July 4, 1442. Once you're back inside the church, look for the CHAPEL OF ST. COSMAS AND ST. DAMIAN, also called the Chapel of "the Relics." Here you'll

R. Fiorentino, Marriage of the Virgin

D. da Settignano, Tabernacle of the Sacrament

Donatello: Pulpit of the Passion; Pulpit of the Resurrection

Old Sacristy

Filippo Lippi, Annunciation, *S. Lorenzo*

Life in the cloister of S. Lorenzo

The Church of San Lorenzo, consecrated in 393, maintained its role as Florence's cathedral for a very long time, until beyond the 7th century by which time the Church of Santa Reparata had already been completed. From the early Middle Ages the Laurentian church was flanked by some buildings adapted as a residence for the canons, probably arranged around a quadrangular cloister, beside the southern side of the church.

Around the end of the 14th century and the beginning of the 15th a second cloister was created following a typically Medieval style of construction, while in about 1450 the original cloister, called the Canons' cloister, was radically transformed, probably the work of Antonio Manetti Ciaccheri, after a design of Michelozzo, at the order of Cosimo the Elder. From 1461 the rooms, divided over two levels and each having a little vegetable garden, began to be assigned to the monks and, some years later, a wall was erected to enclose the entire cloister, subsequently closed by a portal with a dressed stone architrave to which was then added a wooden door that was closed in the evening at the ringing of the bells.

Even today the cloisters of S. Lorenzo still retain unaltered their original appearance and, despite the partial modifications carried out in the following centuries, it is possible to see on the old and very sound plaster along the walls of the ambulatories of the upper floor, from which you can get to the Medici-Laurentian Library, numerous writings, musical compositions and designs, carried out in charcoal or in sanguine, many of which date to before the end of the 15th century.

Among these 'graffitti' should be highlighted a coat of arms of the Pazzi family, a caricature profile that from the quality of its execution could be attributed to Michelangelo's circle, a design for a balustrade with columns (perhaps for the Tribune of the Relics) and a relief for the gable of the door of the mattress maker (who lived in the cloister) this also being attributable to Buonarroti.

Inside the cloister religious life was regulated by strict monastic rules: there was a kitchen and a communal refectory, a room where the chapter met, a church and a sacristy for masses meant for the canons, an archive and various service annexes. The garden was cultivated for vegetables, and farmyard animals were raised there.

The rooms were assigned, with the exception of the prior's, on the basis of the seniority of the priests who, although they paid a rent, had to commit not to carry out modifications, not to light fires, and for reasons of decency, to entertain only their closest family and a minimum number of servants. Entry was prohibited to women (with the exception of the clerics' mothers) and in addition it was forbidden in the cloister to carry out commercial activities, to play games (card games or ball games) or to hang out washing. The presence of some outsiders has been documented over the centuries and, from an 18th-century plan, it appears that the vintner and the mattress maker lived there.

The repeated reprimands of the canons and the chaplains, documented in the papers of the Capitular Archives, bear witness however that in reality, the strict monastic rules were frequently infringed in the Laurentian cloisters. During the course of the 17th century there were frequent reminders about the ban on taking in criminals and individuals wanted for gambling debts, a prohibition that was reinforced by the Grand Duke Ferdinando II who sought in all ways possible to limit scandal in what was considered to be the church of the Medici family. But then the repeated warnings aimed at gamblers show that this illicit activity must have been very widespread and practiced both in the cloister and in the homes of the clergy; another curiosity is the prohibition on the clandestine sale of perfumes, creams and ointments that was carried on by the monks of S. Lorenzo.

Finally, let's not forget that from the second half of the 16th century, some famous Florentine artists in A. Allori's circle had a room in the cloister at their disposal where autopsies were carried out on corpses for anatomical research.

P. and F. Tacca, Monument to Ferdinando I

④

find the reliquaries of Lorenzo the Magnificent. MARTELLI CHAPEL: the last in the left nave, it displays the altarpiece by **Filippo Lippi** depicting the *Annunciation.* FIRST CLOISTER - This first cloister, with its garden, contains many tombstones of men of letters and members of noble families.

◇
3 MEDICI-LAURENTIAN LIBRARY (access from the cloister)

Built starting in 1524 by Michelangelo for Pope Clement VII de' Medici so as to house the library begun by Cosimo the Elder. The collection is composed of numerous precious manuscripts including a Greek-Egyptian papyrus (3rd cent. B.C.) and striking illuminated codices. Work was completed in 1568 by Ammannati and Vasari. The READING ROOM has benches and reading desks. Observe the lovely ceiling in inlaid wood (1550) and the terracotta floor with a similar decorative motif.

◇
4 MEDICI CHAPELS (Piazza Madonna degli Aldobrandini, 6)

These include the CHAPEL OF PRINCES and the NEW SACRISTY. This construction was conceived by Cosimo I as a mausoleum intended to commemorate the Medici dynasty. It was completed by M. Nigetti (1644) under Ferdinando I.

First you'll see Buontalenti's CRYPT where 4 niches with the bodies of the Medici and Lorraine Grand Dukes (such as Giovanni of the Black Bands and Anna Maria Luisa) are kept. Underground (open only on special events) you'll see the *Tomb of Cosimo the Elder* by **Verrocchio** and *the tombstone of Donatello.* Walk up the steps and you'll reach the chapels. This oc-

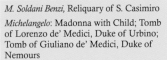

M. Soldani Benzi, Reliquary of S. Casimiro
Michelangelo: Madonna with Child; Tomb of Lorenzo de' Medici, Duke of Urbino; Tomb of Giuliano de' Medici, Duke of Nemours

tagon-shaped room is topped with a dome frescoed in 1828 with *Stories of the Old and New Testaments*. The decorations on the walls, which are covered with semi-precious stones and marble made by the Opificio delle Pietre Dure, are striking. In the splendid, you'll find emblems in semi-precious stones, lapis lazuli, coral, and mother-of-pearl of the Tuscan cities ruled by the Grand Dukes. Members of the Medici family, from Cosimo I to Cosimo III, are buried here. Every sarcophagus was supposed to contain the statue of the prince, but only the ones belonging to Ferdinando I and Cosimo II (in gilt bronze) by P. and F. Tacca were actually made (17th cent.). TREASURE OF LORENZO: near the altar you'll find in 2 rooms the reliquaries, including rock crystal vases, of Lorenzo the Magnificent.

NEW SACRISTY

After passing through a hallway, you'll reach the New Sacristy, which was started in 1520 by Michelangelo. He had been commissioned by Pope Leo X to create an area that would gather the tombs of Lorenzo the Magnificent's family. The work encountered many ups and downs, but was finally completed by Ammannati and Vasari (1555). The room is square-shaped and topped with a dome. Below the *Madonna with Child* (1521) by Michelangelo you'll find the tomb of Lorenzo de' Medici and his brother Giuliano. Next comes the *Monument of Giuliano, Duke of Nemours*, and upon the sarcophagus you'll see the figures of *Day* (on the right) and *Night* (on the left) with symbols representing nighttime like the poppy flower and the screeching owl. On the wall opposite you'll find the *Monument of Lorenzo, Duke of Urbino* (1533), the Magnificent's grandson, depicted as a leader deep in thought. The statues of *Dawn* and *Dusk* rest upon this tomb. An altar with a bronze *Crucifix* attributed to **Giambologna** is also found here.

Canons' menu

Little known aspects of the life of the canons of S. Lorenzo come to light after centuries from the papers in the Capitular Archives. Expense and accounts records describe the banquets prepared for special occasions, such as for 27 September, the day dedicated to Saints Cosma and Damiano, the Medicean patron saints' feast day that began to be celebrated publicly from the return to Florence of the Medici in 1512.

During the course of the 1600s, for this as for other obligatory feasts, a large quantity of different meats was purchased in order to prepare the monastery dinner table properly, such as 'sausages, saucissons, lard, lardon, veal testicles, mutton liver, brain, cockerels, chickens. . .', then some ready made dishes were ordered from the pastry-maker, among them being 'lasagne', 'vermicelli' for soup, fried meat, stewed veal and pies.

The dishes were served together with seasonal vegetables, fennel, radishes, celery, cabbage, etc., and flavored with various spices such as cinnamon, saffron, cloves and rose-water.

The table of the priests of S. Lorenzo also had to have bread, normal and top quality, cheese, parmesan cheese for grating and wine which could be white, red and the liqueur-like 'greco'. The banquet was completed by 'the snow and the ice' to prepare refreshments and to preserve the foods, and the different types of fresh flowers and greenery 'to adorn the table and the refectory'.

For Lent special liturgical calendars were prepared and, preachers came to S. Lorenzo for the occasion from outside Florence, as happened in 1673 for example, with Father Giuseppe da Gubbio. In these circumstances it was necessary to arrange for the purchase of food for the whole of the Lenten period during which, in accordance with Catholic church law, meat was forbidden.

The documents reveal a menu based on fish but hold some unexpected surprises on the ingredients, among which we find caviar, salmon, truffles, oysters, stockfish, anchovy, marinated sole, tuna, dried salted cod, botargo and dried tuna.

C. Munari, Fruit and Musical Instruments, *Uffizi*

The fish dishes were accompanied, as was the case with meat dishes, by an abundance of vegetables such as cauliflower, cardoon, fennel, lettuce, spinach, beetroot, 'weeds and roots', to which though were added some cereals, such as spelt, beans and lupin seeds.

Then once again we find bread, masses of fruit, spices, wine and a sharp citrus jam.

The Lenten period closed with the reappearance on the canons' table of meat to which, in addition to the various types consumed previously for the feasts and referred to above, were added lamb, thrushes and game birds, sweetbreads, corned pork meat etc.

Some rather curious purchases recorded in the 18th century were coffee, chocolate, sugar, lemons, spices, almonds, aniseed, oranges, sweets and candied fruit to which the priests often turned for their journeys out of Florence, when they went to inspect their numerous agricultural holdings that stretched as far as Forlì. To this in the 19th century, was added ice cream, which the priests were accustomed to buying from the shop of the Nistri, right behind the belfries of S. Lorenzo and which they diligently had brought to the monastery during the summer periods.

◇
5 CENACOLO DEL FULIGNO (Via Faenza, 40)

It once was a convent for the nuns of Fuligno. This complex is important because in the refectory or the HALL OF THE CENACOLO, you'll see a lovely *Last Supper*. This is based upon a drawing by **Perugino** and was made by his pupils.

◇
6 PALAZZO MEDICI RICCARDI (Via Cavour, 1)

Today, the Prefecture and various administrative offices are located here. This palazzo was once the residence of the Medici family at the start of their social ascent. In 1437, Cosimo the Elder asked **Michelozzo** di Bartolomeo to build his new residence here. On the façade look for the mullioned windows with the Medici coat-of-arms, whereas at the corners you'll see not only the large Medici coat-of-arms, but also the one of the Riccardi family, who purchased this palazzo in 1659. The Riccardi family enlarged the building by adding a new wing, though maintaining the same types of forms.
COURTYARDS - The first place to visit is the courtyard made by Michelozzo with a portico and Corinthian columns. Here you'll see part of the *Riccardi Collection*, which contains about 300 archeological finds. The second courtyard has now become a garden with statues and lemon trees.

Palazzo Medici Riccardi:
Courtyard of Michelozzo
B. Gozzoli, The Procession of the Magi *(detail)*

CHAPEL OF THE MAGI (✋)

Take the steps on the right (built by G. B. Foggini). You'll arrive in the magnificent CHAPEL OF THE MAGI frescoed by **B. Gozzoli**. This room is square-shaped and has a small tribune for the altar where you'll see an altarpiece depicting the *Nativity*. The walls were decorated with episodes of the *Procession of the Magi*, in relation to the altarpiece image, in 1460. In fact, if you look closely, you'll be able to make out Giuliano, Lorenzo's brother (on the left, the young man riding a horse with a lynx) and Piero the Gouty (portrayed on the right among the group of knights who follow Lorenzo the Magnificent in his gilded armor). Galeazzo Maria Sforza is portrayed on horseback with a gold star on his head, whereas Gozzoli himself is shown wearing a red hat with "Opus Benotii" written on top in gold. Don't miss the HALL "OF THE FOUR SEASONS" with its beautiful 17th-century tapestries, and the typically Baroque GALLERY made by P. M. Baldi; here you can admire the *Madonna with Child* by **Filippo Lippi** (1452 ca.). The RICCARDIAN LIBRARY (entrance from Via de' Gi-

nori, 10) is annexed to the palazzo. Opened to the public in 1715, it gathers approximately 4,000 manuscripts including the illuminated *Virgilio riccardiano*, 700 incunabula, and over 50,000 volumes.

◇
7 CENACOLO DI **S. APOLLONIA** (Via XXVII Aprile, 1)

This room was once the convent refectory of the Benedictine nuns of St. Apollonia (founded in 1339). Once it became State property, in 1891 it was converted into the ANDREA DEL CASTAGNO MUSEUM, an artist who painted the walls with frescoes and sinopie in 1444. Some of the most beautiful scenes include the *Resurrection,* the *Crucifixion*, and the *Last Supper*.

◇
8 CHIOSTRO DELLO SCALZO (Via Cavour, 69)

This cloister gets its name from the cross bearer of the Compagnia dei Disciplinati di S. Giovanni Battista who would walk barefoot during processions. It was frescoed by **A. del Sarto** in the early 1500s with *Stories of St. John the Baptist*. Two scenes were completed by **Franciabigio** in 1518.

◇
1 MARUCELLIAN LIBRARY (Via Cavour, 43)

This important library was established between the 17th and 18th centuries by the abbot of noble origins, Francesco Marucelli. It was opened to the public as early as 1752 and contains an enormous patrimony of circa 554,000 volumes, 2,574 manuscripts, and 30,405 letters and documents.

◇
2 CHURCH OF S. MARCO (Piazza S. Marco)

In 1437, Cosimo the Elder asked Michelozzo to enlarge the primitive 13th-century Romanesque-Gothic convent. It was later consecrated in 1443. Angelico, Fra' Bartolomeo, St. Antonino (Bishop of Florence), and above all the preacher Girolamo Savonarola lived here. The church's façade was altered various times (in 1780 it was adorned in Baroque and late Baroque style). The INTERIOR also underwent many transformations: composed of a single nave, work was done by Giambologna during the 1500s (side chapels), and Silvani modified the tribune and the ceiling in the 1600s. On the COUNTER-FAÇADE, you'll see a *Crucifix* by a pupil of Giotto and on ALTAR I to the right there's *St. Thomas Praying in front of the Crucifix* (1593) by **Santi di Tito**. On ALTAR II, you'll find the *Madonna and Saints* by Baccio della Porta (more commonly known as **Fra' Bartolomeo)**, and on ALTAR IV there's *St. Zanobus*, sculpted by **Giambologna**. In the SACRISTY by Michelozzo, on display are a *sarcophagus* in black marble with a bronze St. Antonino attributed to Giambologna and the *Bishop's vestments of St. Antonino* designed by **A. Allori** (16th cent.). The frescoes of the dome, which was completed in 1712, are by **A. Gherardini**. On the main altar look for a *Crucifix* (1425-1428) by **Angelico**.

Cloister of St. Antonino

From the presbytery you'll reach the Serragli Chapel or the Sacrament Chapel with frescoes by Santi di Tito and **B. Poccetti**. The nave on the left side opens with the Chapel of St. Antonino or the Salviati Chapel, frescoed by **G. B. Baldini**. **Passignano** is credited with the frescoes found in the vestibule. Instead, the bronze bas-reliefs with *Episodes from the Life of St. Antonino* are by Giambologna. Once you're back in the church, visit altar iii and you'll find the tombs of the humanists *Giovanni Pico della Mirandola* and *Poliziano*.

◇
3 MUSEUM OF S. MARCO

A section of the convent was converted into a museum after 1866. You'll reach the museum by passing through the Cloister of St. Antonino, created by Michelozzo and decorated with frescoes depicting *St. Dominic Kneeling in front of Jesus on the Cross* by Beato Angelico. This artist's work can also be seen in the Hall of Hospice, which was once used to host poor pilgrims. Among Angelico's most beautiful works: the *Deposition of Christ* (1432), the *Altarpiece of St. Mark* and of *Annalena*, the *Tabernacle of the Linaioli*, with its lovely 12 musical angels and the treasure closet with 35 images of the *Stories of Christ*. In the Capitular Hall, you'll see a fresco by this same artist that portrays a *Crucifixion and Saints* (1442), as well as a wooden *Crucifix* (1496) by **B. da Montelupo**. Observe the bell known as the "Piagnona" because it sounds like the followers of Savonarola (called Weepers) when he was captured by Medici soldiers in 1498. From here you'll reach the Hall of the Cenacolo frescoed by **D. Ghirlandaio** with the *Last Supper* (1480 ca.). On the ground floor there are other

B. Angelico, Tabernacolo dei Linaioli; Deposition of Christ; Crucifixion and Saints

D. Ghirlandaio, Last Supper

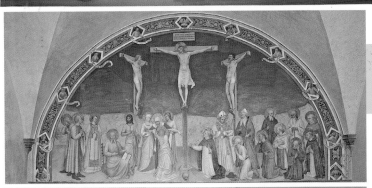

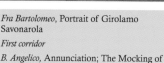

Fra Bartolomeo, Portrait of Girolamo Savonarola

First corridor

B. Angelico, Annunciation; The Mocking of Christ, the Virgin and S. Dominic

Fra Bartolomeo, Altar-piece of the Signoria

Library

Florentine miniaturist, illuminated letter with singing monks

rooms including the HALL OF THE LAVABO with a lunette by P. Uccello, paintings by Fra' Bartolomeo and M. Albertinelli, and the *Madonna with Child* in glazed terracotta by **L. della Robbia**. The HALL OF FRA' BARTOLOMEO is dedicated to this artist who painted the *Last Judgement* (1499) and the *Portrait of Girolamo Savonarola*.

The FLOOR ABOVE is composed of 3 corridors located one after the other around the cloister of St. Antonino. The 43 monk cells are located here. Angelico, assisted by his pupil B. Gozzoli, created a *frescoed cycle* between 1442 and 1445 (the sinopie are probably his) for this area. The most important scenes include the *Annunciation* (signed, 1440 ca.), the *Crucifixion*, the *Crown of Thorns*, *Noli me tangere*, and *Christ Transfigured*. In cell 25, you'll find the *Madonna of the Shadows*. In the THIRD CORRIDOR, **Gozzoli** is attributed with *Christ Is Tempted*, the *Oration in the Garden*, and the *Adoration of the Magi* painted in Cosimo the Elder's private cell. You'll also find the entrance to the LIBRARY where 115 illuminated codices by celebrated artists (including Angelico and D. Ghirlandaio) are displayed in turns.

◇

4 MUSEUM OF NATURAL HISTORY (Via G. La Pira, 4)

This museum derives from the one founded in 1775 by Grand Duke Pietro Leopoldo of Lorraine. The collection is so vast that objects have been grouped into various categories and are displayed in numerous locations throughout the Province. Here you'll find the collections of the MUSEUM OF MINERALOGY AND LITHOGRAPHY (about 45,000 mineral fragments), the MUSEUM OF GEOLOGY AND PALEONTOLOGY (about 300,000 fossil and rock specimens and a Tertiary mammal), and the BOTANICAL MUSEUM (founded

Queens and perfumes

French School of the 16ᵗʰ century, Portrait of Caterina de' Medici, *Palatine Gallery, Pitti Palace*

From the Renaissance onwards, Florence became the European leader in the art of perfumery: it was Caterina de' Medici, who in 1533 married Henry II of Orleans, king of France, that exported to Paris the fashion of wearing perfume, laying the foundation for France's modern-day domination of the world of fragrances.

In the French capital, Caterina didn't want to give up the sophisticated Florentine lifestyle and so took with her Renato Bianco, a famous perfume maker. The accounts show that in Paris the queen at times was home-sick for her far-off Tuscan land and she would then instruct René to prepare fragrant scents that would evoke in her memories of her girlhood. In fact Caterina's preferred perfumed bouquet was prepared with the flowers and plants of the Florentine hills and the Medici gardens.

In Florence the art of perfumery originated in part from the great passion that the Medici nurtured for the sciences of nature and botany, Cosimo I, let's not forget, creating the world's first botanical gardens in Pisa in 1543 and in 1556 in Florence, the famous Giardino dei Semplici whose herbs, together with those from Boboli, were then processed in the Royal Distillery and in the Distillery of the Casino San Marco, veritable alchemists' laboratories, for the preparation of medicines, essences and perfumes.

in 1842 by Filippo Paratore), which is the most important exposition of its kind in Italy.

◇
5 GIARDINO DEI SEMPLICI OR BOTAN-ICAL GARDEN (Via P.A. Micheli, 3, seasonal opening)

This is an open-air museum that extends over 2 hectares. It was created by Cosimo ɪ de' Medici in 1550 and was designed by Tribolo, though it was successively modified. Among the centuries-old trees, don't miss the yew Micheli planted in 1720. Over 6,000 species of plants from across the world can be admired here.

◇
6 ACCADEMIA GALLERY (Via Rica-soli, 60) (☝)

Founded by Pietro Leopoldo in 1784 as a workshop for young Accademia delle Arti students, it gathered only 14th-16th-century Florentine works in so far as they were considered excellent examples of good art. When convents and confraternities were suppressed in the late 1700s, a great number of religious paintings arrived in this gallery, though this practically stopped when **Michelangelo**'s *David* was moved here in 1873. Some of Michelangelo's other masterpieces was acquired during the course of the 20th century. A collection of plaster casts from 19th-century sculptors and of Russian icons from the private collection of the Lorraines were also added.

Accademia Galleria: *Hall of the Colossus; Tribune*

HALL OF THE COLOSSUS - The second of the 9 halls that comprise the museum. Here you'll find the original plaster model of **Giambologna**'s *Rape of the Sabines*. Paintings include the *Mystical Wedding of St. Catherine* by Fra' Bartolomeo and the *Deposition from the Cross* by **Filippino Lippi** and **Perugino**.

Michelangelo: David*;*
Prisoners (Atlas, Young
Slave, Waking Salve,
Bearded Slave)

GALLERY - Michelangelo's four *Prisoners* (1530 ca.) are located here. These unfinished sculptures were intended for the great mausoleum of Pope Julius II in Rome. However, Michelangelo's nephew gave these works to Grand Duke Cosimo I who placed them inside Buontalenti's grotto in the Boboli Garden. They were later moved to the Gallery. The subjects of the statues are: the *Young Slave* and the *Bearded Slave* on the right, and the *Waking Slave* and *Atlas* on the left. To the right of these *Prisoners* you'll also find *St. Matthew*, placed here in 1831; this sculpture was part of an unfinished series of Apostles that were supposed to be placed inside the chorus chapels of the Duomo. You can also admire the *Pietà di Palestrina* (1550 ca.); however, there is still some uncertainty regarding the attribution of this work.

The *David* is located at the back of the Gallery in the neo-classical tribune that was made to house it (1882). This grandiose statue (4.10 meters h.) was sculpted by Michelangelo (1501-1504). The image of David was chosen because it has always been a symbol of Florence and it represents shrewdness that defeats brute force. This work was intended for the Tribune in the Duomo, but it was instead placed in front of Palazzo Vecchio as a reminder of civil and political liberties. In the arms of this Tribune, you'll also find other works including the *Venus and Cupid* (1535 ca.) by **Pontormo** (but designed by Michelangelo). *Christ Entering Jerusalem* by **Santi di Tito** and the *Disputa over the Immaculate Conception* by **C. Portelli** are also worth seeing.

FLORENTINE ROOMS - Fifteenth-century Florentine paintings are on dis-

play here. Look especially for the majestic *Cassone Adimari* (*Dance Scene*) by **Scheggia** with the accurate reproduction of a wedding procession around the Baptistery, the *Thebaid* attributed to **P. Uccello,** the *Madonna with Child, St. John the Baptist, and Two Angels* (1468 ca.) by **Botticelli**, and the soave *Madonna of the Sea* attributed to Filippino Lippi. The *Resurrection* by **R. del Garbo** is among the most important altarpieces on display here.

THE BARTOLINI COLLECTION OF PLASTER CASTS - This room was set up in 1985 with the signed plaster casts created by Lorenzo Bartolini, the most important sculpture teacher at the Accademia di Belle Arti during the 19th century.

GIOTTESQUE HALL - Also referred to as the "Byzantine" hall because you'll find pre-Giottesque paintings here. Observe the lovely panel depicting the *Tree of Life* by **P. di Buonaguida** and the 22 tiles by **T. Gaddi** designed around 1333 and once found in the Church of S. Croce.

TOP FLOOR ROOMS - Set up in 1985, these 4 rooms gather Florentine paintings from the 14th to 15th centuries such as the *Annunciation* and the predella for the altarpiece of S. Trinita by **L. Monaco** as well as the Gothic-style *Annunciation* by the **Maestro della Madonna di Strauss**. Room III contains the collection of Russian icons that once belonged to the Lorraines. On the ground floor you'll find the EXPOSITION OF MUSICAL INSTRUMENTS of the Luigi Cherubini Conservatory (adjacent to the Accademia), which includes rare pieces that belonged to the Medici and the Lorraines. A must-see: the precious Stradivarius violins.

◇
7 Museum and Opificio delle Pietre Dure (Via degli Alfani, 78)

The Opificio, or workshop, was established in 1588 by Ferdinando I de' Medici. It was moved from the Uffizi to its present-day location in 1796. Here you'll find works in semi-precious stone and *scagliola* as well as inlaid mosaics. An interesting collection of rocks is also displayed.

Work desk with wooden tools and showcases with stones, detail of a lathe in the form of Atlas
Cabinet door with sunflower

Opificio delle Pietre Dure

The Opificio delle Pietre Dure is a museum that is both unique and absolutely peculiar to Florentine art. The love and tradition for this type of manufacturing dates back to the early Renaissance.

Born at the Medici court, the passion for objects in semi-precious stones can be seen as early as the 15th century in prized collections of cameos and ancient gems and vases. In the 16th century, the Grand Duke founded a workshop in order to revive this typically Florentine form of art.

In 1588, Ferdinando I established the "Galleria dei lavori" (Gallery of Works). Initially, various Milanese masters specialized in cutting rock crystal worked here, but later on Florentines and other artisans from Northern Europe were admitted. It was a veritable melting pot of artistic styles.

The Grand-Ducal Gallery soon refined the art of the "commesso," or rather, mosaics made with semi-precious stones cut up into various shapes and sizes and then arranged with such precision that the finished object would resemble "a painting in stone."

Tables, cabinets, jewelry boxes, chessboards, paintings, and ecclesiastical objects (a sublime example is the Prince's Chapel) were painstakingly executed with very thin pieces of semi-precious stones. Still lifes, landscapes, portraits, genre scenes, coats-of-arms took shape as differently colored stone chips were placed next to one another. In fact, the skilled artisans of these inlaid mosaics played with the effects the color combinations produced. The objects became even more precious as they were assembled and finished off by artisans specialized in working with bronze, enamel, and ebony.

Over the centuries, the Gallery's creations enriched the Medici residences, but rulers from the most important courts in Europe also coveted these precious objects, which became status symbols. The art of the "commesso," therefore, distinguished Florentine art in the world; it was a symbol of the power and prestige of the Medici, and afterwards of the Hapsburg-Lorraines, who ruled Tuscany beginning in 1737.

The Opificio kept up production until the late 1800s. It then began restoring works of art. The Museum is born from the history of this magnificent place and the people who worked here. In addition to important objects in inlaid mosaic, the Museum displays various collections of rare stones the Grand Dukes intended for the use of the Opificio, drawings, models, and instruments for working semi-precious stones. All these bear witness to 3 unforgettable centuries of art history.

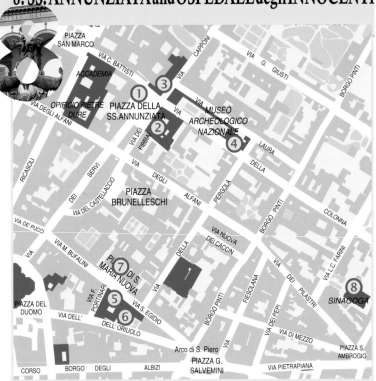

◇
1 PIAZZA SS. ANNUNZIATA

This area was an important center for social gatherings as early as the 13th century. In fact, the weekly market (on Saturdays), the feast of the Annunciation (March 25, which also corresponded to the beginning of the Florentine year), and the popular "Rificolona" (festivities in honor of Mary's birth that are still held on the night between September 7 and 8. According to tradition, worshipers pay homage to the Virgin by entering the church with a wooden pole and an attached lantern) were all held here. At the center of the square you'll find the *Equestrian Statue of Grand Duke Ferdinando I* (1608), begun by **Giambologna** and completed by **P. Tacca**. There are also two fountains with sea monsters (1629) by Tacca. Brunelleschi re-elaborated the square during the second-half of the 1400s. He designed the two loggias that set off the church: the loggia of the Ospedale degli Innocenti (1419) and the one opposite the Confraternità dei Servi di Maria, also called the *Loggiato dei Serviti* (begun in 1516 and designed by A. da Sangallo the Elder and B. d'Agnolo).

☺ **EQUESTRIAN STATUE OF GRAND DUKE FERDINANDO I**

Tradition holds that on the Grand Ducal coat of arms positioned on the statue's plinth designed by Giambologna, on the side facing the church, it is impossible to determine the exact number of bees depicted. In fact they are very strangely arranged around the queen bee and a popular adage ensures good luck to anyone who can count them without touching them.

◇ 2 Ospedale degli Innocenti

On the right of the square you'll find the institute, important in past centuries, that educated children who had been abandoned in the "rota," a rotating stone located at the opposite end of the portico. Begun in 1419 and financed by the powerful Silk Guild, the Ospedale was inaugurated in 1445. The architect created a perfect symmetry for the portico spaces. In 1487, 8 tondos in white and blue glazed terracotta by A. della Robbia portraying newborn babies in swaddling bands were placed in the pendentives between the arches. The vault and the lunettes were frescoed by B. Poccetti.

Cloister of Men - This cloister, completed in 1470, leads to the picture gallery. Observe the decorations with the emblems of the Silk Guild (door), the hospital of S. Maria della Scala (stairs), and the Hospital of S. Gallo (rooster).

Picture Gallery - Here you can admire mostly sacred works: the *Madonna with Child and an Angel* by a young **Botticelli**, the *Madonna with Child* (1450) in glazed terracotta by L. della Robbia, and the *Madonna degli Innocenti* by **F. Granacci**.

Botticelli, Madonna and Child and an angel

D. Ghirlandaio, Adoration of the Magi

Cloister of the Ex-Votos

146

Founded in 1250 by the friars of the Servi di Maria order, it was intended as a small oratory dedicated to Mary. It was later enlarged (1444-1477) and given a round domed, tribune begun by Michelozzo and completed by L. B. Alberti. Under the portico you'll find 3 doors: the one in the middle will lead you to the CLOISTER OF THE EX-VOTOS; here, ex-votos were hung up until 1780. Also observe the gallery of Renaissance frescoes: the *Nativity of Mary* (1514) and the *Arrival of the Magi* (1511) by **A. del Sarto** as well as the *Marriage of Mary* (1513) by **Franciabigio**, the *Visitation* (1514-1516) by **Pontormo**, and the *Assumption* (1517) by **R. Fiorentino**. Two bronze stoups by **A. Susini** (1615) and the *Stories of S. Filippo Benizzi* by A. del Sarto can also be admired.

INTERIOR - It has a single nave and is mainly Baroque in style, especially its decorations: on the ceiling you'll find a painting (*Our Lady of the Assumption*) by **Volterrano** (1664-1670). Try to visit, on your left, the CHAPEL OF

A. del Castagno, The Holy Trinity and St. Jerome, St. Paula, and St. Eustace

B. Bandinelli, Christ supported by Nicodemus

Chapel of the Annunciation

A. del Sarto, Madonna del Sacco

8

OUR LADY OF THE ASSUMPTION, with its marble, small-temple shape and bronze gate. Here you'll also find many ex-votos and a particular silver altar where the *Annunciation* is displayed (this was especially venerated by married couples because it supposedly brought good luck). Other chapels you should try to see include, in the LEFT TRANSEPT, CHAPELS II and III with frescoes (1456) by **A. del Castagno** depicting *S. Giuliano*; CHAPEL IV with the *Last Judgement* by **A. Allori**; CHAPEL V and the *Assumption of Mary* by **P. Perugino**. In the CHAPEL OF RELICS, on the right towards the sacristy, you'll see the tomb of the artist Passignano, who decorated this chapel and was buried here in 1638. Observe the PRESBYTERY and its round tribune shape and 9 chapels (designed by Michelozzo). The decoration is Baroque and the ciborium and the silver frontals on the main altar are rather splendid. Under the choir in the chapel you'll see two *angels* by **Empoli**; in CHAPEL IV, there's the *Resurrection* by **A. Bronzino**. CHAPEL V, also called the MADONNA DEL SOCCORSO CHAPEL, is entirely dedicated to the works of Giambologna. In the RIGHT TRANSEPT, CHAPEL VIII, observe the *Crucifix* (1450 ca.) attributed to A. del Castagno and the marble sculpture group of the *Pietà* by **B. Bandinelli**, who is buried here and who portrayed himself in the figure of Nicodemus. There are also many funerary monuments such as the *Tomb of Marquis Luigi Tempi* (1849) by **U. Cambi,** the tomb and bust of **G. Stradano** (1605), and the *Funerary Monument of Bishop Angelo Marzi Medici* (1546) by **F. da Sangallo**.

CLOISTER OF THE DEAD - You'll arrive here from the left transept (please ask the sexton first). The lunette frescoes with *Stories of the Servants of Mary* were executed by various artists including Poccetti. **A. del Sarto** is credited with the lovely *Madonna del Sacco* (1525) located above the church entrance.

CHAPEL OF THE COMPAGNIA DI S. LUCA - To the right of the cloister; the Compagnia was a 14th-century institution of Italian and foreign artists. In 1563, Cosimo I gave it the title of Accademia delle arti del Disegno, which was located here until 1784. In the vestibule, observe the wooden *Crucifix* by **A. da Sangallo**, while inside you'll see on the altar *St. Luke Painting the Madonna* by **G. Vasari**. On the right observe the *Trinity* by **A. Bronzino**, and on the left, the *Madonna with Child and Saints* by **Pontormo**.

A city of animals

World famous for its art and for the ingeniousness of its citizens, Florence was also inhabited over the course of the centuries by numerous animals, that also contributed significantly to the city's development. Horses, asses, mules and oxen provided the power for drawing tons and tons of marble, stone, earth and wood used in construction and in the creation of the great works which we still admire today. In this regard in the inner courtyard of Palazzo Pitti, under the left colonnade, there is a moving monument dedicated to a mule depicted in the very act of transporting heavy burdens needed for the construction of the royal palace, while a plaque on the parapet of the Arno in Piazza de' Giudici is dedicated to the horse of the Venetian ambassador, Carlo Cappello.

A vital role was played in Florence by cats, which could always be found in churches, monasteries and noble buildings because of their invaluable ability to catch rats. Plump on scraps from the kitchens, the felines led a peaceful life in the warmth of the household hearth, while for those in the churches there was always tripe, which appears in the ancient documents among the fixed expenses of the sacristy. After passing on to a better life, the cat was still useful to man: its tail was used as an effective tool for dusting pictures, sculptures and ecclesiastical furnishings and its skin could be put to various uses, although some were not considered proper, as cardinal Alessandro de' Medici reminds the chaplains of the Collegiate Church of S. Lorenzo in connection with the prohibition on 'skinning cats, squirrels or foxes' for making the 'gufo', a special fur cloak worn by canons.

Dogs were also often welcomed in the churches; locked in the holy buildings at night they acted as guards and deterred any thieves or vagabonds. A dog's usefulness, like that of its enemy the cat, knew no bounds: in the 17th century their skin was used to make soft gloves which are often mentioned in the inventories of the Medici Guardaroba.

Famous dogs have at times been the pretext for a totally original view of the city: around 1850 for example, Virginia Woolf's celebrated *Flush* follows an unusual scent trail that leads it to discover particular scents and picturesque spots of the city that would otherwise have been forgotten.

Flying creatures instead, were unwelcome guests, because as happens today, they often made it extremely difficult to keep the churches and buildings clean. For example, for centuries numerous bats lived in the darkest corners of the dome of the Duomo, until they were completely exterminated during the course of the 1800s by the use of sulfur. During the same period an attempt was made to limit the number of pigeons that populated the skies of Florence and that soiled disgracefully the city's most symbolic buildings with their defecations.

Many other animals appear in important city monuments: the famous bronze piglet, or rather a boar, a copy of a classical sculpture created by Pietro Tacca in 1633 and which can be seen in the Loggia

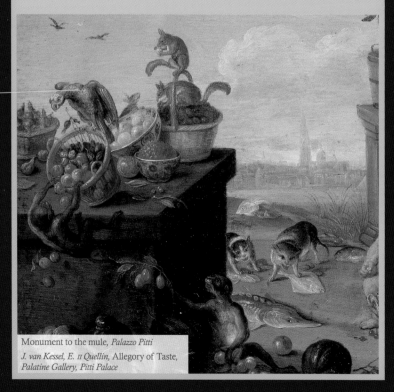

Monument to the mule, *Palazzo Pitti*
J. van Kessel, E. ıı Quellin, Allegory of Taste, *Palatine Gallery, Pitti Palace*

phibians that recreate its natural habitat; the horned head of the cow that sticks out from the side of S. Maria del Fiore, like other similar creatures (visible only through binoculars, though), the famous 'Marzocco' lion, the turtle and the snail of the Dwarf Morgante (in Boboli and the Bargello respectively), and then the bees of the monument to Ferdinando I in Piazza SS. Annunziata, the numerous horses of equestrian statues, the eagles, lambs and still other animals of numerous coats of arms and insignias.

Special mention should be made of the animals in the parks of the Medici country houses. There was the rhinoceros that lived in the menagerie of Boboli, the peacocks and the turtles and tortoises of Poggio a Caiano, and the creatures that populated the estates of the Grand Duchy such as fallow deer, pheasants, foxes, pine martens, weasels, polecats, stone martens, wild cats, gray partridges, partridges, fig-peckers, thrushes, and roe-deer, the hunting of which was strictly regulated.

Of importance to scientific knowledge were the animals that were collected and ordered for the Museum of Natural History, founded in Florence in 1775; mammals, birds and fishes and further tens of thousands of shells, whale bones, elephant tusks, sharks' teeth and many other curiosities which can still be seen today at the museum.

Finally, the original little sculptures in the shapes of animals that were used to decorate the tables during royal banquets, or to be covered with pastry or icing for creating spectacular dishes are also interesting. In 1588, for example, in the expenses of the Medici Guardaroba are recorded various payments to sculptors for the creation of models of animals intended for Coriolano, the court confectioner, some in bronze, such as a fawn, five dogs, a hare, a bull, a bear and a 'wild

Il porcellino, Loggia del Mercato Nuovo
V. Cioli, The Dwarf Morgante, Boboli Garden
Panel with a parrot on the branch of a pear tree, Museum of the Opificio delle Pietre Dure
Equestrian Statue of Grand Duke Ferdinando I

models of animals intended for Coriolano, the court confectioner, some in bronze, such as a fawn, five dogs, a hare, a bull, a bear and a 'wild and prickly boar', and others in wax, such as birds, snails, parrots and fishes; occasionally bas-reliefs were also created, such as for example in 1592, when the confectioner coated a slab depicting 'Fiorenza with a lion at her feet' with quince jam.

4 NATIONAL ARCHEOLOGICAL MUSEUM (Via della Colonna, 38)

Located in the *Palazzo della Crocetta*, built by G. Parigi in 1619-1621 for Grand Duchess Maria Maddalena of Austria. This collection is the most important in Italy for its Etruscan finds and is second, after the National Archeological Museum in Turin, for its Egyptian artifacts. In the garden, admire some Etruscan tombs (like *tholoi* and chamber tombs) re-constructed with material found in the early 1900s.

ETRUSCAN MUSEUM

This collection was begun by Cosimo the Elder and Lorenzo the Magnificent and includes gems, works in bronze, and coins. Many donations and acquisitions over the centuries greatly enriched the collection. The ground floor is dedicated to the ETRUSCAN-GREEK-ROMAN ANTIQUARIUM where you'll see many Etruscan funerary sculptures. Also on display: the *François Vase*, an Attic *krater* (540-530 B.C.), the cinerary urn *Mater Matuta* (460-450 B.C), who was the goddess of maternity and fertility, and the *Sarcophagus of Larthia Seianti* (2nd cent. B.C.), depicted as she brushes aside her veil to look at herself in a mirror. In the rooms dedicated to ETRUSCAN FUNERARY SCULPTURE, finds mostly from Volterra, Chiusi, and Perugina are displayed. You can't miss the numerous urns, especially the *Sarcophagus of the Amazons* (4th cent. B.C.) in marble. Observe also the famous *Small Idol* statue represent-

Sarcophagus of Larthia Seianthi

Sarcophagus of the priest Khonsumes

Chimera

Statuette

The Haranguer

ing a young libating man and the celebrated *Chimera* (4ᵗʰ-5ᵗʰ cent. B.C.), a three-headed monster with a lion's body found in Arezzo in 1553. The Etruscan statue depicting the *Haranguer* (early 1ˢᵗ cent. B.C.) is also noteworthy. The CERAMICS COLLECTION, which gathers Greek and Etruscan vases with black and red figures, and the GLYPTIC COLLECTION, containing Roman and Renaissance cameos and Hellenic and Roman gems, are also worth seeing.

EGYPTIAN MUSEUM

This museum was established between 1824 and 1828 by Leopoldo II of Lorraine. The collection was later enriched and presently contains over 15,000 finds.

Objects are arranged according to date and area of provenance. The time period ranges from prehistory to the late New Kingdom. Don't miss the *Shery Stone Slab* (2500-2200 B.C.) and the *Hippopotamus*, a symbol of fertility. The *Head of Queen Tiy*, wife of Amenophis III (1403-1365 B.C.), is from Karnak. Funerary objects include the *Wooden Cart* from the necropolis of Thebes. The *Bas-relief of the Goddess Maat* dates to the New Kingdom. The section dedicated to funerary papyri with chapters and scenes from the *Book of the Dead* is rather impressive. The *Funeral Trousseau of Amenhotpe* and the *Heart Beetles* date to the 18ᵗʰ-19ᵗʰ dynasties, whereas the 2 stele with an indication of when the tomb was purchased date to the Ptolemaic period.

G. Utens, Belvedere with Pitti, *"Firenze com'era" Museum*

◇
5 FLORENTINE MUSEUM AND INSTITUTE OF PREHISTORY (Via S. Egidio, 21)

Established in 1946, the collections date from the Stone Age and come from excavations in Europe, Africa, America, and Asia. Here you'll find tools made in stone or bone, ceramics, bronze and copper weapons, and the remains of plants and animals.

◇
6 "FIRENZE COM'ERA" MUSEUM (Via dell'Oriuolo, 24)

This museum was established in 1908 and was later moved to its current location. It documents Florence's evolution and transformation over the centuries. It chiefly gathers lapidary fragments from the various demolitions of the city's historic center, drawings, prints, photos, and etchings. Numerous works are on display and include the 19th-century painting *Map known as "della Catena"* (1470), a map of Florence by **S. Buonsignori,** the 12 *Views of Medici Villas* (1599), tempera on panel by **G. Utens**, the 24 prints with *Views of the City* (1754), and 50 others with *Views of Florentine Villas* (1744) by **G. Zocchi**.

◇
7 OSPEDALE DI S. MARIA NUOVA (Piazza S. Maria Nuova)

The oldest hospital in the city still in operation, it was founded in 1288 by Folco Portinari, father of Beatrice, Dante's beloved. Originally it was divided into two areas and had 200 beds. Its interior, with rooms frescoed by N. Gerini at the beginning of the 1400s, was enlarged after a design of Buontalenti with cloisters and an arcade.

In the colonnade at the front, note the busts of Cosimo II and Ferdinando II, and the *frescoes* (1614) of **Pomarancio**. From here you can reach the CHURCH OF S. EGIDIO, inside which are the remains of the *Tomb of Folco Portinari*, the marble *Tabernacle* (1450) by **B. Rossellino** with the original door by **Ghiberti**, and at altar II to the left the *Deposition* by **A. Allori**.

◇
8 SYNAGOGUE AND MUSEUM OF JEWISH ART AND HISTORY (Via Luigi Carlo Farini, 4)

A work from the end of the 1800s by the architects **M. Falcini**, **V. Micheli**

and **M. Treves**, it is a travertine building surmounted by a large dome of copper plates and surrounded by a large garden. Look for the Byzantine-Moorish style mosaics in the interior, and the large marble plaques in the courtyard commemorating the Jews deported during the Second World War.

In the nearby MUSEUM OF JEWISH ART AND HISTORY of Florence you'll see textile furnishings and jewelry for Jewish ceremonies, parchments and antique codices.

If you get a chance, try to visit the CHURCH OF S. MARIA MADDALENA DEI PAZZI (13th cent.) located in Borgo Pinti, no. 58; it is preceded by a cloister where you can admire frescoes by L. Giordano and a *Crucifixion* by **Perugino** (1496). The TEATRO DELLA PERGOLA (Via della Pergola, 12), inaugurated in 1718, is one of Florence's most prestigious theaters.

9. S. CROCE and the BARGELLO

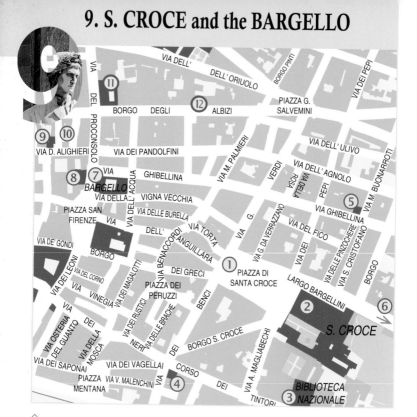

◇
1 PIAZZA S. CROCE

This square was built during the Middle Ages in the area outside the second ring of walls. People would assemble in this piazza to hear sermons given by the Franciscan friars or to participate in public events and games, like jousts or soccer matches (even today the entertaining games of the Calcio Storico Fiorentino are held here every June). Lovely Renaissance palazzos surround the square: *Palazzo Cocchi-Serristori* (no. 1) by G. da Sangallo and *Palazzo dell'Antella* (on the right) with its long façade frescoed in 1620 by artists such as Passignano and Rosselli. You'll also find the family's coat-of-arms and a bust of Cosimo I. Further below you should also see the marble disk (1565) that marked the middle of the soccer field.

◇
2 BASILICA OF S. CROCE (👆)

This church is considered the greatest expression of Florentine Gothic architecture. A. di Cambio began working on the church in 1294, but it was consecrated in 1442. In 1566, Vasari intervened drastically on the interior. In 1874, Baccani erected the bell tower. The basilica's neo-Gothic façade (1863) is the work of N. Matas (his tomb is located inside). On the sides of the church you can still see the original stone covering with its characteristic drainpipes shaped like human and lion heads. On the steps that lead to the basilica you'll find **E. Pazzi**'s statue of *Dante* facing the square (1865).

The INTERIOR, in the form of an Egyptian cross, is divided into 3 naves by octagonal pillars. The central nave has a ceiling with trusses. Numerous chapels belonging to prominent families are found in the transept. The basilica has al-

158

ways been an important burial site for illustrious men. If you start at the counter-façade, you'll find the *Monument to Gino Capponi* (1884) and the *Monument to G.B. Niccolini* (1883). In the right nave: the *Tomb of Michelangelo* (1564) designed by **Vasari**, and in front, the *Madonna del Latte* (1478) by **A. Rossellino**. Next come the *Cenotaph of Dante Alighieri* (1829) and the neo-classical *Monument to Vittorio Alfieri* (1810) by **A. Canova**, with the statue of a *Weeping Italy*. Look for the splendid pulpit by **B. da Maiano** with tiles depicting *Scenes from the Life of St. Francis*. After ALTAR IV you'll reach the *Tomb of Niccolò Machiavelli* (1787) with the allegorical figure of *Diplomacy*. Also visit ALTAR V to see **Donatello**'s *Annunciation* (1433 ca.). Further ahead you'll come across **B. Rossellino**'s *Monument to Leonardo Bruni* (1445-1450), which served as a model for monumental tombs. Finally, the monuments to *Gioacchino Rossini* (1900) and *Ugo Foscolo* (1939) shouldn't be missed. ALTAR VI displays *Christ Entering Jerusalem* (1604) by **Cigoli**.

RIGHT TRANSEPT - The family chapels begin here. The CASTELLANI CHAPEL (the tertiary order would assemble here) was frescoed by **A. Gaddi** (1385) with the lives of saints. The BARONCELLI CHAPEL was decorated by **T. Gaddi** (1332-1338) with the *Life of the Virgin*. This best-known pupil of Giotto is also responsible for the stained glass window, whereas the polyptych with the *Coronation of the Virgin* was made by the master himself.

Church of S. Croce: *Main Chapel*

Various artists on a design by G. Vasari, The Tomb of Michelangelo

A. Canova, Monument to Vittorio Alfieri

B. da Maiano, Pulpit with Scenes from the Life of St. Francis

Giotto, Coronation of the Virgin

Rinuccini Chapel
Giotto, Funeral of St. Francis *(detail)*,
Bardi Chapel; Assumption of St John the
Evangelist *(detail)*, Peruzzi Chapel

SACRISTY - If you pass through Michelozzo's doorway, you'll reach the room the Pazzi family commissioned. Here you'll find relics and anthem books. The room is frescoed by **S. Aretino** and T. Gaddi (*Crucifixion*). From here you'll reach the RINUCCINI CHAPEL, decorated by **G. da Milano** with *Stories from the Life of Magdalene* and *of the Virgin* (1363-1366). The original gate (1371) is still intact. Further behind, you can access the MEDICI CHAPEL, by Michelozzo, with its splendid altarpiece (*Madonna and Child*) in enameled terracotta by **A. della Robbia**.

Once you're back in the church, stop at the PERUZZI and BARDI CHAPELS, splendidly frescoed by Giotto between 1320 and 1325 with cycles dedicated to *St. John the Baptist* and *St. Francis*. In the Gothic, polygon-shaped MAIN CHAPEL, A. Gaddi's frescoes are dedicated to the story of the *Finding of the True Cross* (the church gets its name from this cycle). In the LEFT TRANSEPT, note the BARDI DI VERNIO CHAPEL frescoed by **M. di Banco** (1340 ca.) with *Stories of St. Sylvester*. Volterrano embellished (1664) the dome of the NICCOLINI CHAPEL, where two paintings by Allori and statues by P. Francavilla are also displayed. The Bardi family also owned another chapel closed off by a gate (1335) in which a wooden *Crucifix* sculpted by Donatello and a *ciborium* with two angels in gilded wood by Vasari can also be admired.

LEFT NAVE - The row of funerary monuments begins again: you'll find the one dedicated to the musician *Luigi Cherubini* and to *Leon Battista Alberti*. ALTAR VI displays the *Pentecost* by **Vasari**. Next comes the the 15th-century tomb of *Carlo Marsuppini*, **D. da Settignano**'s masterpiece.

9

D. da Settignano, *The Tomb of Carlo Marsuppini*

Cimabue, Crucifix

Pazzi Chapel

Giotto, St. Stephen, *Horne Museum*

ALTAR V displays the *Pietà* by **A. Bronzino**, and on the floor you'll find the tomb of *Lorenzo Ghiberti*. On ALTAR IV look for Vasari's *Doubting Thomas*. ALTAR II has the tomb of *Galileo Galilei* with a bust by **G.B. Foggini**.

MUSEUM OF THE OPERA DI S. CROCE (Piazza S. Croce, 16)
This museum is located in the former convent refectory. It was inaugurated in 1900 and contains interesting objects from the church and the convent. In the garden of the FIRST CLOISTER, look for the bronze statue by **H. Moore**, *Warrier*. To the right in the first room, you'll see a *Crucifix* by **Cimabue** (post-1272). This work was seriously damaged in the 1966 flood. In the background, you'll find the large fresco by **T. Gaddi** (1333) with the *Tree of the Cross, Sacred Stories*, and the *Last Supper*, on the side walls there are fragments from the church of the fresco by **A. Orcagna** with the *Triumph of Death*, *Last Judgement*, and *Hell*. To your left: the bronze statue of *St. Ludovic of Tolouse* (1424) by **Donatello**. If you pass through another lovely doorway by B. da Maiano, you'll reach the SECOND CLOISTER, created in 1453 in *pietra serena*. The S. Croce complex concludes with the PAZZI CHAPEL. Begun by Brunelleschi (1429-1430), the chapel was completed after 1470 due to financial problems on the part of the patron, Andrea de' Pazzi. The decorations on the wall present 12 tondos with figures of the *Apostles* in glazed ceramic by **L. della Robbia**.

◇
3 BIBLIOTECA NAZIONALE CENTRALE (Piazza dei Cavalleggeri)
The National Library was completed in 1935 to house the

books that had been collected at the Uffizi starting with Angelo Magliabechi in 1714, through to that time. During the following years other bequests were received, to the extent that today there are about 105 kilometers of shelving to accommodate all the books, manuscripts, codices, letters, incunabula and documents. Moreover, since 1885 a copy of every publication printed in Italy has had to be sent there. Among the most important pieces are the autographs of Galileo, the first known codex (from the first half of the 14th century) of Dante's *Commedia* and letters from Boccaccio and Lorenzo de' Medici.

◇
4 PALAZZO HORNE (Via dei Benci, 6)
This palazzo was built in the late 1400s by Cronaca. It belonged to the Corsi family (cloth merchants). In the early 1900s, it was purchased by the English collector H.P. Horne, Oscar Wilde's friend and great enthusiast of Florentine art. His goal was to re-create a genteel Renaissance residence.

"H.P. HORNE" FOUNDATION MUSEUM
The collection comprises a vast assortment of objects (14th-16th cent.): paintings, sculptures, majolicas, glass objects, coins, documents, manuscripts, printed books. Here you'll find a lovely tondo with the *Holy Family* by **D. Beccafumi**, the *Allegory of Music* by **D. Dossi**, and a beautiful panel with *St. Stephen* by **Giotto**. Don't miss the small throne-shaped inlaid bed (15th cent.) and a sacristy chest in inlaid wood with geometrical motifs (Tuscan manufacture, 15th cent.). A fragment of a chest by **Filippino Lippi** is also impressive (15th cent.).

Casa Buonarroti Museum:
Michelangelo, Madonna of
the Stairs; Battle of the
Centaurs
Casa Buonarroti Gallery

◇
5 CASA BUONARROTI (Via Ghibellina, 70)

In his will, C. Buonarroti expressed his desire to open his house to the public; he wanted to give Florence his private collection, which had started with
Michelangelo (he lived in this house between 1516 and 1525). The museum
was opened in 1859, and the "Casa Buonarroti" Institute was established in
1965. Scholars can consult (by appointment) the well-stocked library and the
collection of 200 drawings by Michelangelo, and visitors can admire the marble relief of the *Battle of the Centaurs* (before 1492) and the *Madonna of the Stairs*
(1492), a bas-relief in marble created by using the *schiacciato* technique.

◇
6 CHURCH OF S. GIUSEPPE (Via S. Giuseppe)

The church was built for the order of the same name in 1519 by Baccio
d'Agnolo, whereas the simple façade dates from later (1759). The interior
is laid out as a hall with side chapels. In chapel II, notice to the right a *triptych* by **T. Gaddi** and a *Crucifix* with which the condemned were accompanied to their death; in chapel III a *Nativity* (1564) by **Santi di Tito**, while
in chapel II to the left there is the *Madonna of the Lily* by **R. del Garbo**.
There's a beautiful Agati organ dating from 1764.

☺ Via dei Malcontenti

During the Middle Ages, on the street overlooked by the church, passed
those condemned to death who, from the BARGELLO (Piazza S. Firenze),
traveled along the old Via della Giustizia arriving at the gallows set up
at the end of what today is called, appropriately, Via de' Malcontenti.

◇
7 PALAZZO AND BARGELLO NATIONAL MUSEUM (Via del Proconsolo, 4)

This building was first erected in 1255 and was initially used as the seat of power of the Captain of Florence. Considered the first permanent seat of the city's institutions, it was completed after some time. In later years, the Podestà and the Council of Justice took up residence here. In 1574, the Bargello, head of police, moved here. As a result, some rooms were converted into prisons and torture and execution areas (convicted persons were hanged from the windows). When the death penalty was abolished in 1782, Leopoldo II of Tuscany was the first (1857) to begin restoring the building; he moved the prisons elsewhere and opened the museum in 1865. Today, the Bargello is considered one of the most important museums in the world for its statue and weapon collections. A church dedicated to Magdalene is annexed to the building. In this church, you'll find the fresco of *Paradise* in which a *Portrait of Dante* by **Giotto** was discovered. The most important parts of the collection include works by Donatello and the donations made by the collectors L. Carrand and G. Franchetti. COURTYARD: porticoed on 3 sides. At the center you'll see a well, which replaced the medieval gallows. The side with the staircase by Neri di Fioravanti (1345) is decorated with coats-of-arms in stone and glazed terracotta. Under the arcade you can admire sculptures by artists like Ammannati and Giambologna, as well as a *cannon* (also called *St. Paul's Cannon* for the saint's head sculpted on the bottom).

The entrance on the east side of the courtyard will lead you to the HALL OF 14TH-CENTURY WORKS where you'll find sculptures such as the *Madonna with Child* by **T. di Camaino** and the *Three Acolytes* by **A. di Cambio**. Next is the HALL

OF MICHELANGELO where you'll see
the unfinished *Pitti Tondo* (1504 ca.)
that portrays Mary with Jesus and
a young St. John the Baptist; then
there's the *Bacchus* (1496-1497), *Bru-
tus*, and the *David-Apollo* (1532).
Works by Ammannati, Bandinelli,
Cellini (look for his lovely *Bust of
Cosimo I*, 1547, cast in bronze), and
Giambologna (his spectacular *Flying Mercury*) are also displayed in
this room. Upstairs in the LOGGIA,
with its 19th-century medieval-in-
spired frescoes, you'll see works from
the 1500s including a series of animals (Giambologna's *Turkey* stands
out). Next is the HALL OF THE GEN-
ERAL COUNCIL or Hall of Donatello.
This room, dedicated to 15th-century
Florentine sculptors, contains many
works by **Donatello** including the famous *Bust-portrait of the Leader Niccolò
da Uzzano* in multicolored terracotta,
the *Marzocco*, a lion (symbol of the

city), and the lovely *Atys-Amor*, a bronze cupid that tramples upon a serpent. The artist's most significant works follow: the bronze *David* (1440-1450) and *St. George*, from Orsanmichele and commissioned by the Guild of Armor and Sword Makers in 1416. **D. da Settignano** is credited with a *Young St. John the Baptist*, while the two tiles (one is by Ghiberti and the other is by Brunelleschi) for the Baptistery door competition depicting the *Sacrifice of Isaac* are also on display. Works by Michelozzo and L. della Robbia are also present.

In the Islamic Hall, objects in metal and ivory, majolicas, jewelry, weapons, and carpets (9th-15th cent.) can be admired.

The Carrand Hall gathers over 3,000 objects from Carrand's collection. A must-see: the *helmet plaque of Agilulf* (6th-7th cent.). There are also rooms dedicated to Andrea and Giovanni della Robbia.

Hall of Small Works in Bronze has a lovely bronze statue, *Hercules and Antaeus,* by **A. Pollaiolo** and the *Ganymede* by **Cellini**. But the room dedicated to Andrea del Verrocchio is worth visiting for the striking bronze *David* (1465 ca.) commissioned by the Medici, the delicate *Lady with the Nosegay*, in marble, and the *Bust of Piero di Lorenzo de' Medici*, in terracotta. Here you'll also see works by other artists such as M. da Fiesole

View of the Verone
Michelangelo, Bacchus
Donatello, David
A. del Pollaiolo, Hercules and Antaeus
Giambologna, Royal Eagle
B. Cellini, Ganymede
Verrocchio, Lady with the Nosegay

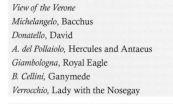

and A. Rossellino. The last room, dedicated to ARMORY, gathers arms of the Medici and from private collections.

◇
8 BADIA FIORENTINA (Via del Proconsolo)

A religious complex founded in 978 for the Benedictines by Willa, mother of Marquis Ugo di Toscana, who is buried here. It was enlarged in Cistercian Gothic style during the 1300s; in 1330, the bell tower was erected. Its interior was completely refurbished in the 1600s, and a new entrance was created on Via Dante Alighieri. The interior is shaped like a Greek cross, and is Baroque in style. Look especially for the *Madonna Appears to St. Bernard* by **Filippino Lippi** on the left wall, while in the left transept you'll find the marble and porphyry *Tomb of Marquis Ugo di Toscana* by **M. da Fiesole**. Through a door to the right of the presbytery you'll reach the evocative CLOISTER OF ORANGES: built by B. Rossellino (1432-1438) with two levels of Ionic columns, it was frescoed on the top part with *Episodes from the Life of St. Benedict*.

9

◇
9 Casa di Dante Museum (Via S. Margherita, 1)
This small museum is located near to the house where Dante was born (today, a well-known restaurant can be found there). The building is a medieval-style reconstruction (early 1900s). Here you'll find documentation on Florence as it was during Dante's life and various editions of the *Divine Comedy*.

Filippino Lippi, Madonna Appears to St. Bernard

◇◇
10 Church of S. Margherita de' Cerchi (Via Santa Margherita)
This little church dating from 1032 is better known as 'Dante and Beatrice's Church', since it was there that Dante for the first time set eyes on his beloved, who was married there, and maybe the supreme poet also got married in this same place. Inside you'll notice the tombstones of the Portinari family, who were the patrons of the church, and among the frescoes an *Enthroned Madonna and Child with Saints* by **L. di Bicci.**

◇◇
11 Palazzo non Finito (Via del Proconsolo, 12)
This palazzo was built for A. Strozzi in rustic ashlar-work in 1593 by Buontalenti who decorated a floor with images of bats and shells. Cigoli fin-

11

G. Vasari, Loggia del Pesce

ished part of the work in 1604 when he built the courtyard. Today, this building is home to the **NATIONAL MUSEUM OF ANTHROPOLOGY AND ETHNOLOGY**, founded by P. Mantegazza in 1869. The material on display comes from the private collections of the Medici. It also contains finds of explorers and navigators such as T. Cook (1779) as well as objects from private collectors like P. Graziosi, who donated his collection to the museum in 1960. These objects are displayed in over 25 rooms, which are arranged according to continent. Visitors can take a veritable trip around the world!

12 BORGO DEGLI ALBIZI

This is an interesting medieval street. It still has many 16th-century palazzos including (no. 26) *Palazzo Ramirez de Montalvo* with graffito work on the façade (based upon a design by Vasari). At no. 18 you'll find *Palazzo Altoviti*, also called Palazzo of the "Visacci" for the 15 marble busts depicting prominent Florentines.

Take some time to also see the **PALAZZO AND CHURCH OF S. FIRENZE** (Piazza S. Firenze) in Baroque style (1645) and the **LOGGIA DEL GRANO** (Via dei Neri-corner Via Castellani), dated 1619 and used as the grain market. It is decorated on the corner by a fountain and by the bust of Cosimo II on the central arch. There's also the **LOGGIA DEL PESCE** (Piazza dei Ciompi), which stands on the site where the famous Ciompi revolt took place (1378). Made by Vasari in 1567, it was intended for the Mercato Vecchio, and is decorated with multicolored terracotta tondos depicting sea creatures and the Medici coat-of-arms. The famous antiques flea market (🖐) is also held nearby.

D. Dossi, Allegory of Hercules, *Uffizi*

Florentine vices

In 1303 Fra' Giordano da Rivalto, preaching from the pulpit of S. Maria Novella, denounced the lack of morality that permeated the Florence of that time: chastity was practically non-existent, marital infidelity rampant, exacerbated by the high number of merchants compelled to spend years at a time away from home, and homosexuality was spreading everywhere.

Anyway, the clerics were the best informed on the intimate and secret practices of the Florentines since in Medieval times the practice of the confession was carried out following a well-defined procedure, similar to a full-scale interrogation, that was so detailed that at times it led even the confessors themselves into temptation.

But no invective was capable of limiting the sexual appetite of a society that was satiated and sophisticated, constantly seeking pleasure; indeed, the 'flesh trade', that the authorities were trying to limit and control, multiplied continuously.

Up to the end of the 1200s prostitution was carried on in the taverns and brothels using strict contracts that bound the women to their masters. Prostitutes were viewed in much the same way as carriers of the plague: forced to make themselves recognizable by covering their head and carrying tinkling rattles, they were permitted to go out on Mondays only but without ever showing their hands, or wearing the 'pianelle', the shoes that were in vogue at that time. Any who infringed these rules, or who came too close to the city or to places of worship, or who even dressed as a man in order to please a client, as was often done back then, were flogged and if they offended again were branded with a red-hot iron on their right cheek.

From the 14th century the concession was made allowing brothels to be opened within the city, in the area of the Mercato Vecchio and, it seems, in the quarters of Santa Croce and Santo Spirito, but only from the 1400s did a more tolerant climate become established which viewed prostitution as one of the city's lesser evils. In fact a demographic collapse, fewer marriages and a rise in homosexuality worried the authorities, including the church, to such an extent as to convince them of the need to increase the unions between men and women.

To defend public morality the Ufficio dell'Onestà, or Office of Integrity, was set up in 1403 (and as a reminder of it there remains to this day a lane with the same name near Orsanmichele) that had among its main objectives the creation of a 'red light' district in the heart of Florence. The area selected, partially walled, was close to the Mercato Vecchio (today the Piazza della Repubblica), where there was already the largest public bordello, branching out towards the areas of S. Lorenzo, the Uffizi and Borgo Ognissanti. Here numerous inns, taverns and shops sprang up where it was possible to meet these 'worldly women', among them many foreigners, who showed off their bodies along the streets or even at the windows. But this wasn't the only location set aside for the sex trade, so much so that in time it became ever more widespread and the authorities were never able to confine it to the institutionalized ghettoes.

In Florence sinners, adulterers, or the simply unfortunate who wished to mend their ways could receive a welcome in the monastery of S. Elisabetta or from the Convertite in Via Chiara (Via dei Serragli), from the Compagnia di S. Maria Maddalena (or Society of St. Mary Magdalene), known as the Society of the 'Malmaritate' (or unhappily-married women), in Via della Scala, or from the Convent of Francesco in Via de' Macci. But even the life of women in the convents was not at all easy: in fact, they were forced to live in poverty and destitution because of lack of resources and in addition were often subjected to violent treatment.

Don't forget that in 1786, at the command of Grand Duke Pietro Leopoldo, Tuscany became the first state in Europe to abolish prostitution as well as torture and the death penalty.

It appears that between the Middle Ages and the Renaissance sodomy found its ideal spot in Florence, as attested to by Dante, who damned some of his illustrious fellow citizens for this sin, the foremost being his master

Brunetto Latini, and as confirmed by certain German and French linguistic usages that speak of 'Florentine vice'. The temptations were accentuated by fashion that highlighted male beauty and called for boys to wear a "short corset at the navel, and breeches. . . with a patch at the front and one behind", as advised by Bernardino of Siena from the pulpit of S. Croce around 1427.

The city's liberal climate, accentuated by the restoration of classical values and by the cultural potpourri, favored the spread of this behavior that became widespread across all the social strata of the population; nevertheless from the 1400s it assumed such proportions as to cause alarm which led to harsher punishments and, on the other hand, greater tolerance of female prostitution.

Despite becoming a common practice however, the liberal habits of the Florentines continued to be punishable by law: anonymous accusations became the principal instruments for exposing any 'deviation' but also for slandering and defaming.

Posted by means of the 'tamburi', which were special holes located inside the principal churches and especially in S. Maria del Fiore, from which the messages arrived at the law enforcement offices, these exposures became increasingly numerous, to the extent that it became necessary to set up different offices for checking the information and to keep a watch on public morals, such as for example the Ufficiali di Notte, or the Night Officers.

The enormous number of documents of these offices, now preserved in the State Archive, tell of an extraordinary Florence, occasionally dark but certainly very human.

F. Furini, Hylas and the Nymphs *(detail), Pitti Palace, Palatine Gallery*

◇
1 PIAZZALE MICHELANGELO (*PANORAMIC VIEW)

If you head down Viale dei Colli, built by Poggi as a panoramic area and residential section for the well-to-do classes, you'll reach Piazzale Michelangelo, which will offer you a breathtaking view of the city. A monument to Michelangelo was placed here (1871); it's a copy of the celebrated *David* decorated at the base with statues (also copies) of the Medici tombs in S. Lorenzo. The loggia-café was also built by Poggi and is located on the opposite side of the square; it was originally supposed to be a museum that would house Michelangelo's works.

◇
2 IRIS GARDEN (corner Viale dei Colli and Piazzale Michelangelo)

Opened in 1955, you can visit this splendid garden only during May. On your stroll you'll come across approximately 2,500 types of irises (since 1251 this flower has been the symbol of Florence). Every year the Società Italiana dell'Iris holds a world-wide competition in which an award is given to the person who can obtain an iris with a rich vermilion color just like the one on the Medici coat-of-arms. No one, however, has truly been successful.

◇
3 CHURCH OF S. SALVATORE AL MONTE

Take the stairs behind the loggia-café. Finished in 1504 by Cronaca, on the Mount of Crosses, this church has an unadorned façade. On the gable, observe the emblem of the Arte di Calimala (Guild of Imported Wool Refiners) that commissioned the church. The inside (1 nave with side chapels) was refurbished. Try to visit, in the left transept, the *Deposition of Christ* in glazed terracotta by **G. della Robbia**.

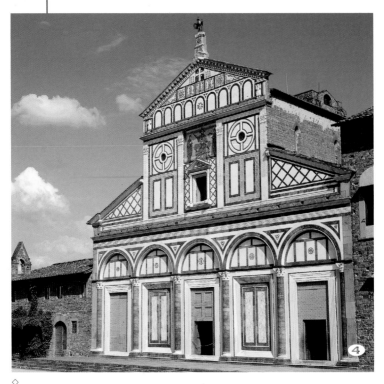

◇
4 CHURCH OF S. MINIATO AL MONTE (🖑) (*PANORAMIC VIEW)

This church rests upon pre-existing Christian constructions. In the 11th century, a Romanesque church dedicated to S. Miniato (he was martyred on this site, 4th cent.) was built here. Initially a Clunaic Benedictine basilica, it then passed to the Olivetan order. The bell tower was rebuilt by B. d'Agnolo in 1524, but it became famous during the 1530 siege of Florence because here Michelangelo set up the cannons that fired against the Imperial troops. It became, in 1552, a fortress. In fact, you can still see the entrance gates: the *de' Medici* gate and the *Soccorso* gate. In 1868, the staircase that connects the church to the Viale dei Colli was designed by Poggi.

The FAÇADE stands out for the contrast of white and green marble that alternate in geometric shapes on two levels: the top level corresponds to the central nave with a window that has a tympanum decorated with a 12th-century mosaic portraying *Christ Enthroned between Mary and St. Miniato*. On the spire observe the gilded copper eagle, the symbol of the Arte di Calimala (patrons of the church, 1401).

The INTERIOR, on 3 levels (crypt, main floor, raised presbytery), is divided into 3 naves by columns. The triumphal arch and the semi-circular apse bear innovative decorations, whereas the embellishment on the walls dates back to the 19th century. At the back of the central nave (the floor has marble inlays, 1207), you'll find the CRUCIFIX CHAPEL made by **Michelozzo** for Piero de' Medici (1448) with panels by **A. Gaddi** and coffers by the Della Robbia workshop in glazed terracotta on the barrel vault.

You'll arrive in the SACRISTY from the presbytery. It is square-shaped with a vault and large lunettes frescoed by **S. Aretino** with *Scenes from the Life of St. Benedict*. Go back into the presbytery and observe on the right an altar with a panel depicting the *Episodes of the Life of St. Miniato* (1320) by **J. del Casentino**. Observe the marble enclosure with transenna, the choir with inlaid wooden seats, the pulpit, and the main altar with a glazed terracotta *Crucifix* attributed to L. della Robbia.

The CRYPT (12th cent.) is the oldest part of the church and is covered with cross vaults that rest upon 36 small columns made of different material (marble, *pietra serena*, terracotta) gilded in 1342. T. Gaddi is credited with the frescoes with a gold background on the vaults.

CHAPEL OF THE PORTUGUESE CARDINAL - You'll arrive here from the left nave. It was built by Manetti in 1466. Its vault is decorated with 4 medallions in glazed terracotta by L. della Robbia that depict the *Cardinal Virtues*. The marble funerary monument was sculpted by the Rossellino brothers; frescoes adorn the walls and include the *Annunciation* (1466) by **A. Baldovinetti**. Next to the church you'll find the MONUMENTAL CEMETERY or cemetery of the "Holy Gates" begun in 1865 for the city's most prominent families. C. Lorenzini (Carlo Collodi) is also buried here.

Mosaicist, 13th cent., Christ Enthroned between Mary and St. Miniato, *detail*

Chapel of the Portuguese Cardinal

Crucifix Chapel

Florentine artists, Pulpit

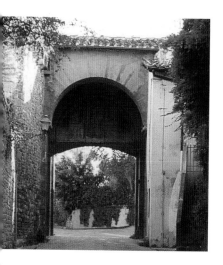

◇ 5 VIA DI S. LEONARDO

A picturesque road leading to the Forte Belvedere. Many artists lived in houses along this road, including the musician Tchaikovsky and the painter O. Rosai. You'll also find the CHURCH OF S. LEONARDO, an 11th-12th-century rural parish. It was refurbished in 1929 and contains a 13th-century marble *pulpit* from which Dante and Boccaccio spoke when it was located in the Church of S. Piero a Scheraggio before being demolished.

◇ 6 FORTE BELVEDERE OR S. GIORGIO
(open during exhibitions)

It was built in 1590 by Buontalenti for Ferdinando I. It was used as a defensive fort from attacks outside the city's walls, which can still be seen nearby. It overlooks and is connected to the Boboli Garden. Don't miss the breathtaking view of the city. (*PANORAMIC VIEW)

At the center you'll see the *Palazzina di Belvedere* (1570), built upon a design attributed to Ammannati.

◇ 7 COSTA S. GIORGIO

Once you've passed the S. Giorgio Gate, which was once part of the second ring of walls, you'll come across a steep descent and one of the city's most characteristic streets, until you reach Via dei Bardi by passing along Costa Scarpuccia. At no. 17 of Costa S. Giorgio you'll see Galileo's house, decorated with his family's coats-of-arms and his bust on the façade.

◇ 8 VIA DE' BARDI

Once called the "Pitiglioso" section of town because greedy, stingy people lived here, it is divided into 2 parts: a more modern section towards Ponte Vecchio and the other towards S. Niccolò, closed off by

lovely 14ᵗʰ-century palazzos that belonged to the most important merchant families. These include *Palazzo Capponi* (nos. 36-38), built for the banker Niccolò da Uzzano. The series of residences is interrupted by the Costa Scarpuccia *terre plein* support, which Cosimo I commissioned in 1547 after a disastrous landslide that destroyed various buildings. A plaque commemorates this tragic event. Right in front of the wall you'll find the CHURCH OF S. LUCIA DE' MAGNOLI or of the "Ruined," founded in 1078 and refurbished various times. Look for the panel with the *Madonna and Saints*, Florentine school (16ᵗʰ cent.), on the main altar. A tabernacle on the outside commemorates St. Francis who also stopped here.

S. Giorgio Gate
Ruins of the 14ᵗʰ-century walls with the Mascherino Tower

9 BARDINI MUSEUM (Piazza dei Mozzi, 1)

This museum is currently being refurbished. It was established in 1881 in one of the 3 residences that belonged to the Bardini family (wealthy merchants). Stefano Bardini, a collector and antiques dealer, was an important figure in the late 1800s. In 1922, he left the Municipality of Florence his entire collection. The architecture of the residence itself is quite curious and includes decorative elements from various periods. Observe the altar dedicated to Augustus that depicts Dionysus (reused as a well-curb), a 12th-century capital with the *Nativity*, and the *Charity* marble sculpture by **T. da Camaino**. Don't miss the fireplaces and the Roman bath in porphyry as well as the Persian carpets and the rooms dedicated to armory. The works in terracotta are also interesting and include the *Madonna with Child*, attributed to **Donatello**, and the *Madonna dei Cordai* (by this same artist). You'll also find the CORSI GALLERY in this museum, donated to the Municipality of Florence in 1937; it gathers over 600 works from the 12th to 19th centuries. Near the museum you'll see the **BARDINI GARDENS** (Via dei Bardi, 1r), purchased in 1913 by S. Bardini. It is one of the most representative models of Italian-style gardens with a panoramic terrace overlooking the city. (*PANORAMIC VIEW)

10 S. NICCOLÒ GATE (Piazza G. Poggi)

The area created in 1866 by Poggi includes the centuries-old crenellated gate of S. Niccolò at the center. This gate was built in 1324 as a rampart along with the walls in order to defend this part of the city. It

is the only original gate left in Florence. As you enter, you'll find a fresco with the *Madonna and Saints* (15th cent.). From here you can walk up the 2 flights of steps built by Poggi and reach Piazzale Michelangelo after passing lovely grottos and fountains.

11 S. Miniato Gate

This 14th-century gate with a walkway on the wall that is supported by arches can be crossed as you go to the Church of S. Miniato a Monte, along Via del Monte alle Croci (also called the *Via Crucis,* built by the Franciscans).

12 Villa di Poggio Imperiale (Piazzale di Poggio Imperiale, 1)

Following the avenue that goes out from the Porta Romana you arrive at this 17th-century villa, built by G. Parigi for the Grand Duchess Maria Maddalena of Austria. Remodeled between the 1700s and the 1800s in the neo-classical style (notice the façade with a balcony topped by a gable), the villa was the residence of the Medici and the Lorraine until in 1865, King Vittorio Emanuele of Savoy transformed it into the girls' boarding school of the SS. Annunziata, an exclusive school for the education of young aristocrats from all over Europe. The interior *frescoes* were carried out by Florentine artists of the 1600s and by ornamentalists of the 1700s who added the Chinese style decorations, while the original furnishings have been retained.

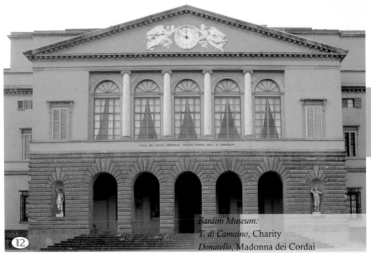

Bardini Museum:
T. di Camaino, Charity
Donatello, Madonna dei Cordai

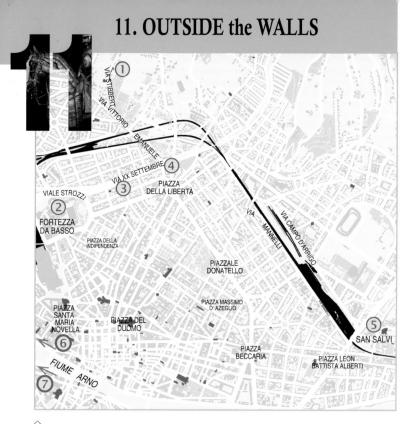

11. OUTSIDE the WALLS

◇
1 STIBBERT MUSEUM (Via Federico Stibbert, 26)

Nestled in a lovely park, this museum gathers one of the most important private collections in the world of centuries-old weapons and costumes. The collector was Frederick (or Federico) Stibbert, who was born in Florence (1838-1906); his father was English and his mother was Florentine. Heir to a vast patrimony, Federico stood out for his eclecticism: he was a painter, a member of the Florentine Accademia delle Belle Arti, a businessman, and a writer. Thanks to his incessant traveling, Stibbert was able to gather over 50,000 objects (from late 15th century to first Empire). His collection was then bequeathed to the British government who in turn donated it to Florence. In 1908, a foundation was established. Stibbert refurbished and enlarged his residence in order to house his collection and make it available to the public. Today, the museum is composed of over 60 rooms, including his family's living quarters. Stibbert's intention was to re-create surroundings and furnishings suited to the collections on display. The most interesting objects are mentioned below, though keep in mind that their location in the museum may be subject to change.

ORIENTAL HALLS (6-8) - Gather Turkish and Persian weaponry and armor, *Turkmen suits of armor* (15th-19th cent.), and splendid *Indian weaponry and armor* (16th-18th cent.).

CAVALCADE HALL (9) with its Italian, German, and Ottoman *train of knights* (16th-17th cent.); in the STANZINO (small storage room, 11), you'll find the *German funerary corselet* of Giovanni of the Black Bands. As you're in the PASSAGEWAY (17), observe the *saber* of Gioacchino Murat, while in the MILITARY HALL (18), you'll

Cavalcade Hall

find the *flag* of the second infantry regiment of the Kingdom of Italy.

COSTUME HALLS (38-41) - This collection is one of the most complete and richest in Europe and contains very rare pieces. Observe the male and female costumes as well as the liveries and accessories (16th-18th cent.). The FREDERICK STIBBERT ROOM (48) still has its original furniture, with mementos of his family and portraits. In the EMPIRE HALL (49), which belonged to his mother Giulia, you'll see the *ball gown* of a lady-in-waiting at the court of Elisa Baciocchi. In the EMPIRE LOGGETTA (50), you'll find the *Grand Costume of Italy* that Napoleon Bonaparte wore when he was crowned King of Italy in 1805.

JAPANESE ROOMS (55-58) - Observe the splendid *samurai group*, as well as the Japanese and Chinese weapons, helmets, and gear. Don't miss the painting collection, especially those by J. Suttermans, Bronzino, A. Allori, G.B. Tiepolo, and L. Giordano, and the collection of everyday objects such as clocks and watches, combs, cutlery, ceramics, fans, canes, and umbrellas. This villa is surrounded by a wonderful English-style romantic park designed by Poggi. Here you'll find a pond with a small Egyptian-style temple and obelisk, a small Hellenic-style temple, and a greenhouse with rare exotic essences.

◇
2 FORTEZZA DA BASSO OR OF S. GIOVANNI

This fortress was built beginning in 1534 and was designed by A. da Sangallo the Younger for Alessandro de' Medici who feared internal strife more than outside invasion. Shaped like a pentagon, it takes up a vast area where today important events and exhibitions are held. Observe the keep, covered in *pietra forte*, and the octagonal guardhouse.

Table with top in malachite
Knight Armor
German funerary corselet of Giovanni of the Black Bands
Napoleon's Grand Costume of Italy

◇
3 RUSSIAN-ORTHODOX CHURCH (Via Leone x, 8)

It was built thanks especially to the donations of the Demidoff Russian princes during the early 1900s. It was designed by the architect M. Preobrazenskij and consecrated on November 8, 1903. It is square in shape and made of *pietra serena* with a base in *pietra forte*; its domes are made with Russian-style multicolored ceramics and are topped by bronze crosses. The inside is adorned with stuccos, reliefs, icons, and paintings by G. Lolli. Czar Nicolas II donated the Carrara marble iconostasis.

◇
4 PIAZZA DELLA LIBERTÀ

Designed in the late 1800s by Poggi in Florentine Renaissance style. At the center you'll find the S. GALLO GATE (1285) with tabernacles decorated with lions and a 16th-century fresco in the lunette depicting the *Madonna, Child, and Saints*. On the north side you'll see the *Triumphal Arch of Francesco Stefano of Lorraine,* erected on the occasion of his entry into the city in 1739, topped by the *equestrian Monument of Francesco Stefano* by **G. B. Foggini**.

◇
5 COMPLEX OF S. MICHELE A S. SALVI (Via di S. Salvi, 16)

This religious complex is composed of the monastery of S. Salvi and the Church of S. Michele a S. Salvi, which dates back to 1048. The CENACOLO DI ANDREA DEL SARTO MUSEUM was set up in the former refectory in 1981. The room was frescoed by the artist in 1527 with the *Last Supper*; legend has it that this work was spared by the soldiers of Charles V because it was so extraordinarily beautiful. The museum also gathers other works by this artist including the *Annunciation* (1509 ca.) and the *Pietà* (1520 ca.). You'll also find paintings by R. del Garbo, Pontormo, and Vasari.

◇
6 PARCO DELLE CASCINE

The largest public park in the city, it is more than 3 kilometers long and covers 118 hectares; it derives its name from the farms that the Medici had here in the 1500s for raising cattle. Later trees were planted, a botanical garden was laid out and tree-lined paths laid down for holding court par-

Cathedral of S. Romolo

centuries-old ecclesiastical objects are displayed. In the 13th-century CRYPT, a granite *Baptismal Font* (1569) by **F. del Tadda** is located on the right.

BANDINI MUSEUM (Via G. Duprè, 1)
Opened to the public in 1913, this museum houses the canon Angelo Maria Bandini's collection, which was bequeathed to the Bishop and the Chapter of Fiesole in 1803. This collection is mostly made up of Florentine paintings and sculptures (1200s-1400s) as well as other objects and sculptures of later centuries, including many pieces by the Della Robbia workshop. Artists include T. Gaddi, B. Daddi, N. and J. di Cione, J. del Sellaio, L. Monaco.

ARCHEOLOGICAL AREA (Via Marini, 1) (*PANORAMIC VIEW)
This area includes a THEATER, which is still used during the summer, built at the time of Augustus; it can seat 3,000 people and is 34 meters in diameter. Situated on the side of the hill, the theater is divided into 4 sectors by 3 flights of steps. The stage in front of the orchestra is supported by a small wall. To the side you can see the niche that once held the puller used to raise and lower the curtain. The BATHS, which also date back to the time of Augustus, are near the theater, but are marked off by the Etruscan walls. The ROMAN TEMPLE, rebuilt after a fire in the 1st century B.C., has a tympanum adorned with terracotta figures and a staircase with 7 steps. Observe the ruins of the 5 columns that held up the portico. The ETRUSCAN TEMPLE, built during the 3rd century B.C., was dedicated to a divinity that brought health and wellbeing; the flight of steps and the remains of the roof decorations (now at the Civic Museum) are still visible.

CIVIC MUSEUM - Founded in 1873, it displays objects and finds from the Etruscan, Roman, and Medieval periods found in and around Fiesole. Among
the most interesting works: cinerary urns, found in Etruscan tombs (2nd-3rd
cent. B.C.) from the nearby Via del Bargellino, bronze statuettes portraying
animals and humans, glass wine chalices used by the Langobards, ceramics.
Don't miss the stele in *pietra serena* with scenes of a banquet, dancing, and
hunting (first-half, 5th cent. B.C.). Since 1985 the A. Costantini Collection,
donated to the Municipality of Fiesole, has been housed in the ANTIQUARIUM
COSTANTINI (Via Portigiani, 9). It comprises about 170 objects in ceramic
from Attica, Etruruia, and Magna Graecia.

PRIMO CONTI FOUNDATION (Via G. Duprè, 18)
In the 16th-century *Villa le Coste*, you'll find the archive and collection of
the painter P. Conti who passed away in 1988. He is buried in the chapel
(located in the garden), decorated with paintings from the late 1600s.

HILL OF ST. FRANCIS (Via di S. Francesco)
If you travel up the steep hill, you'll reach the *Garden of Remembrance*, which
offers a breathtaking view of Florence. (*PANORAMIC VIEW) Continue along
and you'll arrive at the hill that in ancient times was the Etruscan-Roman
acropolis. Here you'll see a religious complex composed of the Basilica of S.
Alessandro, the Church of S. Francesco, and the Church of S. Cecilia.
The most interesting of the three is the CHURCH OF S. FRANCESCO. Built in the
1300s for the Florentine women hermits, it passed to the Franciscans later
that century. It was refurbished in the early 1900s, though it still maintains its

12

Roman Theater
Church of S. Francesco

15th-century façade and a portion of its left side. The INTERIOR (a single nave) contains many works including the *Annunciation* by R. del Garbo on ALTAR II to the left. In the CHAPEL OF S. ANTONIO, there's the *Manger Scene* in terracotta by the Della Robbia workshop. From the 15th-century cloister, near the sacristy, you'll reach the MISSIONARY MUSEUM OF ETHNOGRAPHY, which contains Etruscan and Chinese objects as well as an Egyptian mummy.

◇
4 FOOTBALL MUSEUM (Viale Palazzeschi, 20 – Coverciano)
Established in 2000 as a center for documenting the history of the game of football (soccer), it contains memorabilia (footballs, shirts, scarves) and the trophies won by the national team at the World Cups, at the Olympics and at the European Championships. There's an excellent multi-media section with videos and photographs. Close to the Museum is the Italian Football Federation Technical Center (Via G. D'Annunzio, 138), that hosts the retreats of the players of the national team before important matches.

◇
5 GALLUZZO CHARTERHOUSE (entrance Buca di Certosa, 2) (🖐)
Along the Via Senese, you'll find the Charterhouse that dominates, from Mount Acuto (110 meters), the Val d'Ema. This monastery was founded in 1342 by will of N. Acciaioli; it was later enlarged and embellished thanks to the bequests of many noble Florentine families. In 1810, following French suppression, the monastery also possessed a rich library (now completely lost) and over 500 works of art. Among the works currently housed in the PICTURE GALLERY: 5 large lunettes with *Episodes of the Passion* (1525) by **Pon-**

tormo. The CHURCH OF S. LORENZO and the CHURCH OF MONKS (both dating to the 14th cent.) are also part of the complex, and inside you'll find works by Florentine and Tuscan artists (1500s-1600s). Don't miss the splendid inlaid walnut stalls (late 16th cent.) in the second church.

MAIN CLOISTER - Built in the early 16th century, its architecture is Renaissance in style. In the arch pendentives, there are 66 busts in glazed terracotta (apostles, saints, evangelists, and figures from the Old Testament) from the G. della Robbia workshop. On three sides of the cloister you'll see various monk cells, each of which also had a vegetable patch.

◇
6 VILLA DEMIDOFF-PRATOLINO AND PARK (Via Bolognese, seasonal opening)
If you continue along highway 65 (direction: Bologna), you'll reach this immense park that today belongs to the Province of Florence. The land was purchased in 1568 by Francesco I de' Medici who asked Buonatalenti to build a villa and a garden with grottoes, fountains, and statues. Over the following years, it became one of the most important sites for cultural events in Florence, and in 1683 concerts by Scarlatti and Händel were held here. The villa was demolished in 1824 under the Lorraines, but the immense park was spared. In 1872, the Savoy family sold the property to the Demidoffs, who then erected a new villa. The most important work is the *Apennine* fountain (1589) by **Giambologna**, with its splendid grottos. Nearby you'll also see a stone dragon by G. B. Foggini. Don't miss *Cupid's Grotto* (1577) and the CHAPEL by Buontalenti with its small dome and portico with plaques that commemorate the Demidoff family.